Visit www.AshleyEmmaAuthor.com to download free Amish books (the books may change periodically)

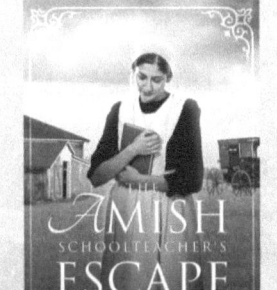

Prequel to Undercover Amish

Free Short Story!

FREYA: AN AMISH SHORT STORY (Book 1 in the Freya Series)

Get Freya here on Amazon for free or search Amazon for "Freya by Ashley Emma": https://www.amazon.com/Freya-Amish-Short-Ashley-Emma-ebook/dp/B01MSP03UX

Check out my author Facebook page at www.facebook.com/AshleyEmmaAuthor to see rare photos from when I lived with the Amish in Unity, Maine

ASHLEY'S AMISH ADVENTURES:

AN OUTSIDER LIVING WITH THE AMISH

"May God guide us both, for eternity is so long..."
-An Amish friend from Kentucky

Ashley Emma

Other books by Ashley Emma on Amazon

Coming 2019:

COMING AUTUMN 2018: AMISH AMNESIA

Amish Amnesia (Covert Police Detectives Unit book 3)
Freya (Book 3)
The Ring Thief
Amish Twin Sisters: Prequel to The Ring Thief
Princess and the Amish Pauper: the Amish Fairytale Series

Cover Design by Cormar Covers.

ASHLEY'S AMISH ADVENTURES

Copyright © 2016 by Ashley Emma

All rights reserved.

No part of this book may be copied, shared, or used without the author's permission.

All rights reserved. No part of this book may be reproduced in any manner, except for brief quotations in critical articles or reviews, without permission.

Praise for *Ashley's Amish Adventures*

"A refreshing glimpse inside Ashley Emma's writing process. Reading about her in-depth, genuine curiosity and appreciation for the people she met on her adventure into the Amish community felt like an intimate behind-the-scenes tour."

--Marie Schaeller, bestselling author of *Breaking the Chains of Silence*

http://www.Marieschaeller.com

*

"Emma Ashley is a brilliant author. I admire her work. I was wondering what it is like to be Amish and also what it is like to be inside an Amish community. Through her books, she leads the readers into an unknown environment. She does it in a way that does not make me feel lost or left all by myself. She holds the reader's hand all along through the story. Therefore, I recommend you to get a tour with Emma Ashley in her Amish world."

--Ndeye Labadens, multi-bestselling author of *African Memories: Travels into the Interior of Africa, Secrets Book Launch Journey to the Ultimate Success, Relocation without Dislocation: Make New Friends and Keep the Old,* and *Australian Memories: Discover the Aussie Land and the Mysterious Red Center*

*

"An intriguing and riveting read! This book gives readers a very rare peek into life in an Amish community. The author personally immersed herself into the Amish life, in order to authentically portray their passion for contentment, simplicity, and faith as the setting for an adventure of a lifetime. While it is an easy read, it is very intriguing and riveting! The author has a way of drawing a reader into every scene and keeping the momentum going. The characters she introduces us to are so real and relatable, despite the fact that they live such distinct lives from what would be considered main stream modern America! In fact, there is a sense of envy that causes an inevitable reflection on what we consider to be necessary and essential in our daily lives. It was a refreshing read!"

--Tracy Lee, author and pastor

*

"An amazing read, and I thank the author for sharing her story and experience living with the Amish. It removes the mystery of the Amish, and how they live without the many amenities, we take for granted. There is much we could all learn from them and most certainly recommend reading this book."

-Marlene Wagner, author

www.attractloveatanyage.com

https://www.facebook.com/coach.marlenew

http://marlenewagnercoaching.leadpages.co/free-dating-strategies-report

*

"I LOVE these Amish books by Ashley Emma. They not only grab your interest and keep you reading, they give you a feel like you know a few Amish people and care about them. This is the most powerful step to understanding a culture different from your own. Thanks, Ashley, you have broadened my horizons and you made it fun on the way! There is also a homespun gentleness and honesty about the spiritual side of these differences. If everyone acted like this, Christianity would have a better world view and there would be less hatred in the world. There is nothing more we could ask for from a few books!"

--Chris McKay Pierce, author of *Customer Service can be Murder*

Author's Note and Some Important Information:

This is a 100% true account of my time in the Amish community in Unity, Maine. All the people in this book are people I met during my stay there. All last names have respectfully been left out or changed. I did not embellish this story in any way. It is completely factual.

Please note that even though most of this book is written in past tense to make it easier to read, most of the information in this book is still current. Some present tense writing will be mixed in with past tense writing so it makes more sense.

I apologize if some of the photos are blurry. These photos were taken back when I had an old cell phone that did not have a good camera on it. I couldn't afford a good quality camera at the time.

I wrote this journal back when I was twenty years old, so the "voice" or writing style of this book may reflect that fact in this genuine, unique inside look into the Amish lifestyle. (However, the book has been thoroughly edited to improve the writing while still maintaining its voice.)

To read the continuing story don't miss the second book in this series, Ashley's Amish Adventures: Attending an Amish Wedding!

Click here to get 3 free eBooks and get all of Ashley's future books for free at ashleyemmaauthor.com.

Now, enjoy the experience as you join me on my Amish adventures!

-Ashley Emma

To my mom, Susan, who started all of this.
Thanks for the books about the Amish…and thanks for everything.

To David, the love of my life, for encouraging me the most.

CONTENTS

November 9th, 2011 1

Sunday, February 5th, 2011 4

Wednesday, February 23rd, 2011 5

February 27th, 2011 9

March 5th, 2011 11

Tuesday, October 18th, 2011 46

Saturday, October 22nd, 2011 47

Sunday, October 23rd, 2011 53

Monday, October 24th, 2011 59

Tuesday, October 25th, 2011 65

Wednesday, October 26th, 2011 72

Thursday, October 27th, 2011 89

Friday, October 28th, 2011 98

Letters to and from the Amish 108

October 16th, 2011 110

October 7th, 2011 111

November 2011 112

December 2011 114

December 31, 2011 116

January 30th, 2012 119

Excerpt from Undercover Amish 130

    Chapter One 130

    Chapter Two 139

About the Author: 156

November 9th, 2011

A Note about the Amish

When I was fourteen I wrote a manuscript about traveling back in time because I imagined what it would be like, but I never thought I'd come close to experiencing something that incredible. But when I lived with the Amish, it was almost like traveling back in time.

To do research for my bestselling Amish novel, Undercover Amish, and my upcoming novel The Ring Thief, I lived with three Amish families and have visited them several times over the past few years. This book is the product of all my research, adventures, and experiences I had while living in the Amish community of Unity, Maine.

I did not originally plan on writing a book about my research, but so many of my readers wanted to know what it was like for me to live in an Old Order Amish community, so I decided to write this documentary.

While I was in the Amish community of Unity, Maine to observe their culture, I did not stand on the sidelines. I dressed like them, got my hands dirty, and did everything they did. I wanted the entire Amish experience that Charlotte, the main character in The Ring Thief, would have as she left everything she knew to take refuge and hide with her younger sister in an Old Order Amish community, afraid for their lives after traumatic experiences.

The Amish are a truly amazing, kind, and smart group of people, as you will discover in this book. The Amish church began hundreds of years ago, but the Amish today are not very different from the church founders.

The only things many people know (or think they know) about the Amish are what they have learned from TV, movies, or Amish romance novels. These can sometimes stereotype or falsely portray the Amish. In fact, my Amish friends in Unity choose not to read Amish love stories for this reason. Hopefully this work will help break some of these stereotypes.

In the Bible, God calls his followers to live "separate" from the world. Many Christians think that means merely not doing some things other people do, but the Amish take it literally. In fact, they take many of the things in the Bible literally. The Amish do indeed live separate from the world, not only by their location, but in the way they dress, pray, travel—by virtually every aspect of their lives.

I think the Amish understand and know just as much or even more about the world than *Englishers*, or people who are not Amish. The Amish are hard workers, and family and friendship are so much more important to them than material objects. They do not need possessions to be happy, and believe me, they are happy. I highly respect them.

Growing up, I suppose I knew the Amish dressed in old-fashioned garments, but I didn't know anything else about them. Then about a year ago, my mother gave me some Amish novels. I read several of them. (Later I would learn many of the books I read are banned by Amish parents.) I became completely fascinated with the ways of the Amish. I just wanted to learn more about them.

In case you don't know much about the Amish, here is some basic information. The Amish (not to be confused with Mennonites) live very simple lives. They believe being content with a simple life is important because God looks at the heart, and

God needs to be first in one's life—not possessions. That is why they do not need materialistic things to be happy. There are the Old Order Amish, who live without electricity and vehicles, and there are the New Order Amish, who may own vehicles or use electricity. Each Amish community varies and has different ways and rules.

I wrote my Amish novels based on what I learned about the Old Order Amish community I stayed with in Unity, Maine. I wrote this book from my own observations and experiences with the people I lived with and met there. Much of this book was written in a notebook or on my phone as I lived in Unity. The laptop I owned at the time was a hunk of junk with a very short battery life.

All the characters in my Amish novels are based on wonderful Amish individuals I got to know in Unity. However, though their first names were not changed, all last names have been changed to respect their privacy, even though they did not ask me to do this. They know I write about them. In fact, they read my work and readily approve of it. They were happy to meet a writer who wanted to accurately portray them. Several of the characters in my novels are based on my Amish friends.

Even though I started going to Unity solely to do research for The Ring Thief, my friendship with the Amish blossomed. I hope to return again soon.

I hope you enjoy this book and love learning about the Amish as much as I did and still do. For more Amish reading, check out my new bestselling novel, Undercover Amish.

-Ashley Emma

Sunday, February 5th, 2011

Today I had an idea. I decided to live with the Amish for a while.

I don't want to join the Amish. I just want to research a novel I am going to write. I need to go to a place where I can get away from worldly distractions and learn as much as I can.

I know very little about the Amish. Most of my knowledge comes from fiction-based media, and much of it could be wrong. Immersing myself in their culture will be a crash course in who they are and what they are about. I need to be thrown out of my comfort zone and learn to live without everything I'm used to—electricity, chaos, and shortcuts. I want to know what it's like to leave everything familiar and have to live with a family I don't know in an Amish community. That is going to happen to the main character in *The Ring Thief*, and I want to portray her situation accurately.

I have no idea how I will be able to write when I am there, though. I want to bring my laptop, but it is old and the battery dies so quickly, and I don't know where I will be able to plug it in. I guess I will have to write everything in my notebook or on my phone, if I can find somewhere to charge it, and transfer my writing to my laptop later. I've done it before. My phone battery lasts a lot longer than my laptop battery, and it charges faster.

Wednesday, February 23rd, 2011

Last week I made several phone calls to inquire about living with an Amish family. Since I knew there are plenty of Amish in Pennsylvania, I called Lancaster County first. It would be a long drive for me, but I figured that was the closest Amish community, so I would just have to make the trip.

As the phone rang, I began to have doubts. Would they turn me down? Would my request offend them? Had anyone done this before? If so, how many? Maybe this was a common request after all.

Then someone answered the phone, disrupting my thoughts.

"Hello. I am calling because I would like to live with an Amish family for a short time. I am writing an Amish fiction novel, and I want to accurately depict the Amish lifestyle. I thought the best way to do so was to research a community first-hand and then use my own experiences as a reference. Are there any Amish families who would be willing to take me in for a little while?" My stomach fluttered with nervousness. I was not sure if they would be all right with me writing about them.

"There are several tours where you can come see the Amish community." The man's response was monotone, disinterested. "Many people come here to see the Amish."

"No, I don't want to be a tourist. I want to actually live with them. I want to live like them. I'd work with them, dress like them, and do everything they do. I need to immerse myself in the culture."

"Oh." He sounded much more interested in the conversation. "Are you thinking of joining the Amish?"

Okay, so he hadn't been listening to what I said. He probably fielded a lot of questions about the Amish lifestyle during the day, so I couldn't fault him for that. "No, no. I am really just doing research for a book I'm writing."

There was a slight pause. "Oh. I see this is a Maine number. Do you know there is an Amish community in Maine, in the town of Smyrna?"

"There are Amish communities in Maine? I didn't know that!" Maybe I wouldn't have to travel very far after all.

The man gave me the number to Smyrna. When I called, the man who answered told me about the Amish community in Unity, Maine, which is much closer to where I live. Unity is only two and a half hours away from my house.

He gave me the number to Unity, and I placed my third call. The Amish in Unity do not have phones in their houses, but they do have phones in their businesses. I was given the number to a store, but no one answered. I left a message and awaited a reply.

A few days later, the owner of the store, an Amish man named Caleb, called me back.

"We would love to have you stay at our house. We have seven daughters and one son. The youngest is two and the oldest is eighteen. We have plenty of room here," Caleb told me.

"Wow! Thank you! Do you mind if my mother comes with me?" Even though the Amish are commonly known as a gentle people, and because it is always safer to travel in pairs, I decided to bring my mom with me. I didn't want to travel alone my first time going, and she was more than excited to go. There was no one I would rather take with me, since she was the one who first got me interested in the Amish.

"No, of course not. She is welcome to. We are looking forward to meeting you both."

True, a family of eight children is rather large, but I love big families. "I'm from a big family too. I'm one of six children."

"Well, you will enjoy it here then. Could you come this upcoming Saturday night into Sunday so you could come to church and meet the community?"

"That sounds great!"

Throughout our pleasant phone conversation, I didn't mention I was writing a book about the Amish. I wasn't sure what they would say if I told them. I wasn't trying to be deceitful. I just didn't want them to assume things about me until they met me first. I would wait until I got there and see how it would go.

When I asked Caleb on the phone what we should wear, he said we could wear anything we wanted as long as it was modest and conservative.

"What do the women there wear?" I asked him.

"They wear long dresses and head coverings. We would appreciate it if you dressed modestly, but we do not expect you to cover your hair."

I want to blend in with dresses of our own that were similar to the style of Amish woman's clothing. Later that day my mother, Susie, and I realized we had nothing old fashioned enough to wear, so we went to Goodwill and got long-sleeved, floor-length dresses so we wouldn't stand out too much.

I've heard Amish church services are held in people's homes, are about three hours long, and are spoken in German. I've also heard that the Amish mostly speak Pennsylvania Dutch, a form of German, with their families when they are home. I took German for three years in high school, but since then I've forgotten most of it. However, once I start studying it again, it always comes back to me quickly. I need to start reviewing it.

I got some books at the library today and did some research online about the Amish. I want to know as much as I can about their rules, customs, and lifestyle before I go so I can blend in.

I just can't wait to go to Unity! I hope this experience will really change me for the better and that I learn as much information for my novel as I possibly can.

February 27th, 2011

I am thinking of so many questions about the Amish. Will they mind if I write down the events of the day in my journal? Will they be all right with me going there to learn about their ways so I can write a book about them? Will they let me use their names for characters in the book? Would an Amish man be offended if I shook his hand?

What if I fall asleep during one of their three-hour church services and fall off my chair onto the floor? Someone has done that before in my church. Or worse...what if I do something they consider offensive? Will they care if I use my cell phone? What if it rings at the dinner table?

What if I make one of the teens want to leave the Amish by telling them about the outside world?

What if...what if....

I'm not scared. I'm just getting a little anxious.

I've told some people about my upcoming trip, and sometimes they say how they have visited the Amish country too, usually in places like Lancaster County, which is where everyone thinks I'm going. Many people like to visit to see the plainly dressed people and try to take pictures of them while they go on tours.

"Oh, yes, I visited Lancaster County during our vacation last year with my family, and we stayed in a hotel right outside the Amish community," one woman told me. "It was lovely there."

"No, I am not just visiting or going on vacation. I am going to live with them to do research for a book I am writing. I'm going to dress like them, work with them, and be like one of them for a week," I told her.

"Oh...wow," she said, eyes wide. "That's different. I've never heard of anyone doing such a thing. The Amish will actually let you live with them for a week, even though they don't know you? Do they know you are going to write about them?"

"I haven't told them yet. If they don't want me to write about them in particular, I will just not use their real names. And yes, they're fine with me living with them. It's amazing how trusting they are, actually. I'm not so sure I would let a stranger live with me and my family like that."

Some people tell me that going to live with people I don't know is dangerous. They think it's a scam, and that someone who is not actually Amish called me back and invited me to their house. Some think it's just plain weird, like I expected. Others are saying it's a good thing for me to do. I knew people would think many different things, but I have faith this will work out wonderfully.

I've decided that even though I am going to Unity to research my Amish novels, *Undercover Amish* and *The Ring Thief,* while I am there I will journal everything I do and make that into a documentary. I will call this journal *Ashley's Amish Adventure.* I have started to tell people this, and one thing is for sure—several people cannot wait to read all about it.

March 5th, 2011

I made Mom and myself some bonnet-like head coverings out of white handkerchiefs and ribbon ties today, just in case they ask us to cover our hair. We want to blend in with the Amish as much as we can, but I doubt they will ask us to wear head coverings. They probably won't expect us to do everything like them, but I want to try and make an effort, not just as a courtesy, but because it will help with my research.

The next morning, I put on my brown dress with some plain black boots that we got at Goodwill. Mom wore a green dress that had a pattern on it, and though the Amish do not wear patterns, it was the best we could find.

We packed up the car and left the house with a GPS and a plentiful supply of crackers and yogurt.

Mom had a thought that made me worry. "What if they laugh at us for trying to look like them?"

I hadn't thought of that! My stomach flopped.

About halfway through our drive, we stopped at a gas station for a bathroom break. I started to get out of the car when I realized how I was dressed. I almost didn't go in, but then I put on my long coat and decided to just do it.

A man stopped us at the door. *Oh no, he's going to ask us why we're dressed funny or make fun of us.*

"Sebago Lake!" he exclaimed, reading something on my mom's car. "I won a fishing derby there once!"

Relief washed over me. Maybe he didn't think we were strange at all. Is this how all Amish feel when they leave their community?

Do they do that often? Maybe they don't. And maybe they don't care what people think, anyway. I have a feeling they're secure in who they are. That's probably a refreshing way to live, being unconcerned about the latest fashions and newest releases. It's probably both liberating and grounding.

Or maybe I'm just reading too much into this, and the Amish have the same concerns and feelings we all do.

My stomach churned. There were so many intricate facets to this journey that I hadn't even considered. I had wanted to learn about their culture and way of life, but I hadn't even considered their feelings about it until walking in their shoes. Or dress, as it were. Blending in while learning was already proving emotionally difficult, even though so far it hadn't posed any real problems.

We finished at the gas station and got back on the road. On the way, we got a call from Caleb saying he was leaving his store for about an hour, and he wanted us to wait for him there until he got back. He said his assistant Louis would take care of us until his return.

My mother and I speculated about whether he had a car or if he was taking a horse and buggy. We really had no idea what to expect. I had read that most Amish did not own cars, but I had heard that some New Order do.

To pass the time while we drove, we called a relative to tell her about what we were doing.

She was shocked. "I wouldn't go live with a strange family in this day and age! They could be dangerous! You never know. What if they aren't even Amish and they murder you?"

We tried to explain that I'd done my research and due diligence. I knew they actually were Amish, and I knew how nonviolent the Amish are. We would be completely safe with them. In fact, they are probably some of the safest, gentlest people in the world. I read in an article that there had never been an Amish murderer until the early nineties.

I then realized how surprising it was that Caleb didn't ask me questions like why I wanted to live with them or if I was a Christian. How extraordinary! He trusted God enough to let two strangers into his home and be around his children—without question.

They must have had incredible faith to let strangers into their home.

During the last few miles of our drive to Unity, I excitedly watched for signs of Amish life. So far, everything looked like any other small town. There were run-down gas stations, houses with cars in the driveway, and pizza restaurants. No buggies in sight. Were we in the right place?

We took a turn down a long road. The GPS said we only had a few more miles to go. I started to wonder if we typed in the right address. This looked nothing like what I had expected. Where were the black and white houses and the horses and buggies? Where were the men with beards and hats, and where were the women in long dresses?

I watched for houses with no shutters, no power lines, and no cars outside. I knew Amish houses usually don't have shutters, but they do sometimes have brightly colored curtains in the window.

Though some houses did not have shutters, almost all the houses we passed had cars in the driveway. I started to think the Amish here were New Order and owned vehicles. Had I made a mistake in coming here? I wondered how much information I could use to write my book from Amish who used electricity and cars. That was not really what I wanted for my book. People wanted to read about the Old Order Amish because that lifestyle was so foreign to them.

Just when disappointment settled in, I saw a yellow street sign with a horse and buggy on it.

"Approaching destination," announced the GPS. "Your destination is on the left."

So we were in the right place. The disappointment I'd felt lifted, and a smile crossed my face. This was what I wanted.

To the left of us was a gray house with white shutters. I had always thought Amish houses were black and white. That's what I had seen in movies. Already I learned something, and we hadn't even reached our destination yet.

We found Caleb's community store at the next driveway over and pulled in. "Is this it?" I wondered out loud.

The store resembled a log cabin. It had a metal roof, and there was a large assortment of wooden furniture and bird feeders on the porch. Behind the store were two houses surrounded by wide fields with horses.

I looked around, got out, and followed Mom into the store. A friendly black and brown dog greeted us on the porch. We entered the store and the first thing I noticed was that it was so...eerily quiet.

(Below is a photo of the store taken from down the street.)

(Caleb's house is pictured below and part of the store's porch is on the right of the photo.)

No music played. There were only two other customers in the store.

I never noticed before how much music makes a difference in a public place. I guess I'd grown so used to excess background noise from TV and radio that I usually didn't notice music in stores.

But I noticed its absence in this one.

We approached the young man at the counter, whom Caleb had said would help us. The young man, Louis, said he knew I was coming once I told him my name. Caleb had told him about me.

"How long have you been talking to Caleb?" Louis asked.

I wondered why he asked, but didn't question him. "A few times on the store phone over the last few weeks."

"It's not the store phone," he said. "It's a phone the community shares. Anyway, did Caleb tell you he had a new baby girl a week ago?"

(Below is a photo of the phone shanty the community shares.)

(Below is a photo of some watermelons near the shanty that the Amish grew.)

"No," I answered. "How many children does that make?"

"Nine," Louis answered. "He has eight girls and a boy."

"And I thought six was a lot!" exclaimed my mom.

People always tell us that six children is a lot. To us, it's just family. I couldn't imagine it any other way. I looked forward to meeting Caleb's family. It would be nice to be with a large family again.

We asked Louis a long string of questions, starting with whether or not church was tomorrow.

"Church is every other week, and Sunday School is on the weeks that church is not on. Tomorrow there will be Sunday School, which is like church for everyone, but the service will be from 9 a.m. to 11:30 a.m. There would be a lunch after, and you are certainly welcome to stay. Everyone brings food to share."

He also said the service would be held in English, to our relief, and that church services are usually about three hours long.

Three hours?! Wow. I willingly go to church almost every week, but our services are only about an hour and a half long. At least this Amish service would be in English. I was actually excited to go to church to see what it was like.

I realized Louis was wearing clothes that did not look Amish. He had on a black zip-up vest and a shirt with buttons on it. I thought the Amish did not wear buttons. I had read that in a book.

Maybe he was not Amish. I asked him if he was, and he said yes.

Oh no, they wear clothes that aren't old-fashioned. I hurried out of the store and went inside the car. Mom followed.

"These are the only clothes we brought. They wear modern clothes! We are going to look so stupid!" I said.

Then Mom began to laugh.

"It's not funny!" I wondered what we should do, and even briefly considered driving back to the nearest town and buying some clothes.

Before I made a decision, I remembered I told my best friend, Kate, I would call her when we arrived. I called, but she didn't answer, so I left a message.

"Hi, Kate. We are here, and we are wearing long dresses and they wear modern-looking clothes. My mom won't stop laughing because we didn't bring clothes that we usually wear. They are going to laugh at us!"

My mom laughed even harder.

Just then, a pony wagon rolled by with a few women on it. They wore long dresses, somewhat like ours, along with head coverings!

"Oh, never mind!" I said, still recording a voicemail message. "We just saw a bunch of ladies go by, and we'll fit right in. Sort of."

I hung up, and we went inside the store again.

"Are we dressed appropriately?" my mom forwardly asked Louis.

He chuckled. "You will be fine," he said. "We understand you are not Amish, so you can even wear your regular clothes and we wouldn't mind, but with those clothes you will blend in."

I sighed in relief.

"So, is that Caleb's house over there?" I asked Louis, gesturing toward the gray house next door that we had seen earlier.

"No, Caleb's house is that way, behind the store." He spoke while organizing some things on the counter.

I went to the closest window and looked out. It was set far back into a field, on the edge of the woods, and had a very long, unpaved driveway. The house was tan and had a maroon metal roof. There were no shutters, and of course no power lines. There was a large, tall metal pipe coming out of the roof, like a chimney. It was a very nice, large house. And I had been expecting a small black and white house with an outhouse.

Just as we started talking to Louis again, my phone rang. I wondered if he thought that was rude.

I knew it was Kate calling, so I went outside to talk to her.

"I just got your message. It was hilarious!" she exclaimed.

I told her about the store and how we had asked Louis several questions, and I described Caleb's house. Then I went back inside the store, and my mother and I sat down in handmade rocking chairs from Lancaster County, Pennsylvania. I looked at a bookshelf next to us and read the titles. One of the books was the German *Ausbund*, or songbook, and I looked through it to see if I could understand any of it, but I only understood a few words. I tried to teach some German to my mom. She speaks French fluently, since my family is French (despite the family connection, I speak next to none), but she doesn't know any German.

It didn't matter, though. We would get by while we were here.

A little later, a man came into the store with a teenage girl who wore a long dress and prayer *kapp,* or white head covering that resembles a bonnet. They walked toward us, smiling.

This had to be him. "Are you Caleb?" I asked him.

"Yes, I am. It is nice to meet you, Ashley." He shook my hand then introduced us to the girl, his daughter Beth, who was fifteen. I introduced my mom to them.

"Sorry about the wait," he said. "We had to finish installing the toilet in the building where we will be having church tomorrow."

Oh, good. They had indoor toilets!

"It's okay. We kept ourselves busy and asked Louis a lot of questions. He was very patient with us," my mom said and smiled at him.

"Good. All right, let's go up to the house." He thanked Louis for welcoming us.

(Below are photos of behind Caleb's house.)

(Christina's house and barn are in the photo above. Below is Caleb's house and his barn is on the left.)

(As you can see in the photo below, there is a lot of laundry that is done every week at Caleb's house!)

(Below are some photos of the fields near Caleb's house.)

(The house in the photo below is Caleb's mother's house.)

As we walked outside, my mom offered Caleb and Beth a ride in her car, but they said they would rather walk. So we got in the car and attempted to drive up the driveway, which was extremely slippery. Our car barely made it up. I didn't know how Caleb and Beth walked the whole way without falling.

(Below is a photo of Caleb's barn, some buggies and an old-fashioned Maytag washer.)

An adorable little girl in a prayer *kapp* watched from the house's front window as we approached. We parked, grabbed our bags, and went inside the house. It had taken us so long that we pulled in right after Caleb and Beth reached the house.

When we walked through the door, the first thing I saw were three dark-haired girls in pale blue and gray dresses sitting on a couch beside Caleb's wife, who was holding the newborn baby.

They told us to put our bags by the door, and we put our coats on the sewing machine. I expected white walls and drab décor, but was pleasantly surprised. The room's walls had been painted light blue, and the kitchen's walls were light yellow. To our left was a huge quilt in progress being held up on a wooden contraption that resembled a table with the quilt as the table top. In the corner near the quilt was some sort of nonelectric sewing machine. There was a door leading to what looked like a play room with stuffed animals on a bench. To the right of that was a bookcase with encyclopedias and well-known board games. Straight ahead of me was the couch, which had a blue pattern on it but was covered with a white sheet. There was no clutter. The walls were bare except for a clock and a calendar. There were no pictures, and it was all very clean and organized.

To our right was a long, plastic-topped kitchen table. I could hear chopping sounds and pots and pans clanging. Caleb's daughters bustled around, already making dinner. From where I stood, I could see the back of the gas stove, and I could feel its heat. One of the girls took a lighter from Caleb and lit the gas light above the table, which also gave off heat and surprisingly bright light. One of the other girls brought us chairs that were on wheels but had been covered with plain gray fabric.

We sat down, and all the children were introduced to us. Regina, who is eighteen, is the oldest. Then there is Cara, Beth, Elsie, Rosaline, Mary Esther, Joanna, two-year old Jonas, and baby Emma Sue. Their mother's name was Rosie.

I realized that even though there were so many children in the house, it was very quiet besides the sounds of the girls cooking. There was no TV or radio, of course.

My house, which houses only five people, always has much more commotion than this house with twice as many people.

The girls went back to making dinner while the younger ones quietly read and my mother, Caleb, Rosie, and I talked. Mom and I told them about our family and how we homeschooled. I had gone to Veritas Academy for high school, which only had eight people in it at the time.

Then they asked us what we did for a living. "I'm a cosmetologist," I told them. My mother and I owned a salon together in our home at the time.

"What is that?" Rosie asked, confused.

"Mostly I go to elderly ladies' homes and wash their hair for them if they are unable to. And I cut men's hair," I said, and that was the majority of my job at the time. Since Amish women do not cut their hair, I left out that I do many women's haircuts. I also left out everything else, like hair coloring and highlighting and manicures and pedicures. I wasn't even sure if they would know what those things were.

"So," Caleb asked. "Why are you here? What do you hope to gain out of this experience?"

"I am fascinated with the way the Amish live," I said. "My mom gave me some books to read about a year ago, and ever since then I have wanted to learn more about it."

"There was something about writing a book," Caleb said. So, he had talked to the man I had called in Smyrna. There was no avoiding it. I had to tell him about my book.

"Yes, that's me. I write novels. I want to write a novel about a girl from the city whose parents die, and she has to live with her Amish family she never knew she had." I told them a bit more about *The Ring Thief* storyline.

"See, usually Amish novels don't portray us correctly." Rosie shifted the baby in her arms. "I don't let my daughters read them. They are always about romance." I didn't understand what she meant at the time, but later on I would learn more about the process of Amish dating. Rosie continued, "It is not secretive or scandalous, like in many Amish romance novels. Amish dating is serious, with no physical contact whatsoever, and usually leads to marriage."

"I write Christian novels," I said. "That is why I am here. I want to learn as much as I can about the Amish so I can write my book correctly. I want to get everything right."

"My father was a writer," Caleb said. "He wrote a book called *Give Me This Mountain*. I am glad you have come to research before writing. Usually, as Rosie said, writers do not portray us correctly, but it is wonderful that you have chosen to."

I smiled, relieved. "So, are you all right with me writing about you and your family here? I can change your names, if you want."

"I am fine with that. You don't even have to change our names. I am just happy you have chosen to do this, to write about how we really are," Caleb said, surprising me.

I grinned. Joy bubbled up inside me. I could hardly believe they were fine with me writing about them!

After we talked for a while, Rosie told us we could bring our bags upstairs and see the rest of the house. Regina led us up to the second floor and showed us our room first. It had blue walls, a queen bed, a chest by the window, and a nightstand with a kerosene lamp on it. There was also a closet with spare dresses in it.

(Below is the view from out of the window. You can see part of Caleb's barn on the right.)

Then there was the bathroom. We were happy to see a toilet and a shower, but the sink had not been installed yet. They had been renovating the bathroom recently.

Regina showed us the rest of the girls' rooms. I was surprised to see mirrors and perfume and lotion in their rooms. What was the difference between those things and makeup, which wasn't allowed? My guess was that makeup alters the appearance and lotions and perfumes do not, but I didn't have the courage to ask. I didn't want to sound like I was criticizing their choices. Maybe once I knew them better...

We went back downstairs, and I offered to help with dinner.

"It's all right," Cara said. "You are the guest."

"I want to help. There has to be something I can do." I looked around the busy kitchen full of old-fashioned-looking girls. I had to blink a few times and remember I was still in the twenty-first century.

"We're making egg salad for church tomorrow," Regina said. "If you really want to help, you could peel the eggs."

"Sure!" That was something I knew how to do without electricity. Once I had them all peeled, rinsed, and mashed up for the egg salad, I asked what else was left.

"We just have to mash the potatoes, but I can do it," Regina said.

"I really don't mind doing it," I told her. "I do it at home."

"How do you usually mash potatoes?" Regina asked.

"By hand, with a masher." I wondered if there was some sort of electric potato masher sold in stores. We sure don't have one at my house.

Regina gave me the pot of potatoes. I usually do it the same way they do, except they add cream cheese to theirs, which made them really good.

I knew I'd be making mine like that from then on.

Soon dinner was ready and we set the table. They used plastic dishes that were a cross between bowls and plates. We all sat down, and I realized I forgot to tell my mom they pray silently before dinner. At our house, we usually pray aloud. I hoped she wouldn't be too confused, and she wasn't. She said nothing and went along with it.

After the prayer, we passed the delicious food around the table. The girls made the mashed potatoes, gravy with meat in it, a green bean casserole, and corn. We also ate bread my mom brought with some jelly. I have to say, Rosie's help wasn't necessary with meal preparation. Those girls were great cooks!

They had started making dinner around 4:00 p.m., when we got there, and we finished cleaning up around 7:00 p.m. Dinner was a three-hour event—all without television or music playing in the background or cellphones going off. It was a much slower pace than meals I'm used to, but the food was so good, and we shared some great conversation. It was a pleasant change for me.

After we finished eating, they sang "God Our Father." Mom and I didn't know it, so we just listened, and it was so beautiful. Even the little children sang every word.

Afterward, I helped the girls wash the dishes.

"What do you like to do at home for fun?" Cara asked while she dried a cup.

"I like to draw. Do you draw?"

"Yes, we like to draw."

"What do you draw? Can you draw people?" I asked.

"Yes. I like to draw landscapes and animals though," said Cara. I was surprised they were allowed to draw people, since photographs are not allowed. I wanted to ask the difference, but the kitchen bustled with activity as we all tried to clean up, and the conversation moved on before I got the chance.

After we finished the dishes, Cara asked me if I would read to her younger siblings.

The younger Amish children do not speak much English. They speak only Pennsylvania Dutch until they go to school, and that is when they start to speak English.

While I read to them, I made funny voices for the characters, and I tried to be animated, so they smiled, even if they might have not completely understood what I was saying. As I was reading, I realized how strange it was to see the girls walking around in their long dresses and *kapps*, which I had only seen before on movies or the covers of books or in Amish movies.

Even though their lifestyle is different, we still have a lot in common. We all share many of the same interests and beliefs. If not for the old-fashioned clothes, I would have thought they were any other non-Amish Christian family.

After reading, I learned there was a Singing the next day at 6:00 p.m., but we heard it was supposed to snow at 12:00 p.m.

A Singing is when the community gathers to sing for a few hours, and sometimes Amish boys will give rides home to the girls they like. It is kind of like their way of going on a date.

It all sounded like fun, and I hoped we could go, but the threat of bad weather loomed in my mind.

Mom asked Rosie if there would be coffee in the morning, and Rosie said they made coffee regularly. Mom was very happy about that. She had been wondering whether or not she would get her morning coffee.

We all discussed how we would travel to church in the morning. My mom offered rides in her car, and Caleb said he would let his girls ride in it if they wanted to. He said it is not a sin for us to own a car because we are not Amish, but they believe it is better to own buggies because, for them, it's all about being content with what you have or can make. Though they did not own cars themselves, riding in someone else's car was permitted.

Around 8:00 p.m., we were sent to bed. Caleb gave us a battery-operated stand-up light that resembled a lantern. (See photo below.)

I was not used to going to bed so early. I don't recall sleeping at all that night, and once I heard sounds of feet in the hallway and doors opening and shutting at 6:00 a.m., I was already awake and anxious to get on with the day. I jumped out of bed to get ready for church.

(Below is a photo of the view we could see out our window which I took from my car.)

Afterward, I brought all our bags downstairs and put them in the car because Mom said she was pretty sure we would have to leave right after church before the storm hit. By the time I was done, the girls were done making breakfast. They made toast from the bread Mom had brought on a pan on the wood stove. There was fruit and store-bought cereal, too, in clear plastic containers instead of cereal boxes.

This time before we ate, Caleb prayed aloud, and we sang after we finished eating. I wondered if they only prayed aloud on Sundays. Another question I had but didn't have the opportunity to ask.

We cleaned up from breakfast while Caleb hitched up the buggy.

Mom gave Mary Esther a ride to church in her car. I decided to ride in the buggy with Beth, Joanna, Jonas, and Caleb. Rosie stayed home with the baby, and the rest of the girls walked to church.

Riding in the buggy was a terrifying but fun experience. Caleb made certain sounds and the horse sped up with a jolt. Most of the ride to church was uphill, and I thought we were going to slide backward from the slush and ice, or get stuck. Those buggy wheels are so narrow...sometimes I was sure we were going to tip over. I held onto the seat with white knuckles, and Beth and Joanna playfully laughed with me at my nervousness.

When we arrived, Mom's bright red car stood out from the buggies like a ladybug among ants.

Most of the women wore light or dark blue dresses with buttons in the back. They wore white prayer *kapps* with black *kapps* over them. The black ones were designed to be worn outside. They also wore black sneakers or black boots.

(The finished church and school is pictured above.)

The church building looked like an unfinished house. The windows were not yet installed and were temporarily boarded up, but the wood stove kept the entire building relatively warm. There was a table where the women left their coats and bags.

Suddenly, several of the girls started chattering and pointing out the window. I looked out and saw a gray-haired woman trudging through waist-high snow toward the church, clearly on a mission, walking stick in hand. She finally came around the building and entered. Once she did, she came right up to me. I probably stood right out.

"You must be Ashley. Caleb told me about you. I'm his mother, Elizabeth. Welcome. It is so nice to meet you." She smiled at me, still catching her breath.

"It's nice to meet you too. And now I have no excuse to ever miss church again after seeing you walking so far in such deep snow!"

The other women watched as Caleb's mother introduced herself to my mom. Then a line formed behind her. One by one each woman approached us to introduce themselves until we had met every female in the building. On Sundays the men and women sit separately and do not mingle, so we did not meet any of the men.

As I spoke to more and more people, I realized the Amish in Unity have an accent. Maybe it's more of a northern Maine accent—I'm not sure. They pronounce "really" like "reallay" and "family" like "familay" and they roll their L's a little bit. This became more apparent the more and more I spoke with the Amish.

We went downstairs for the church service. If I wouldn't have known from my research that men sit on the right side and women sit on the left, I might have accidentally sat with the men like my mom almost had. But I steered her to the women's side. I saw a hymnal with the last name of the family I was staying with written on it, and we sat there.

"The women sit in the back and the girls sit in the front usually, but you may sit wherever," said Caleb's mother. We stayed in that seat. As I waited, I looked around the room at the crowd of over seventy plainly-dressed people.

Out of all of them, my mother and I were the only ones who owned cell phones. Isn't that something?

Service began, and we sang from the songbook. Most of the singing was in German. A man would call out a song number, and we would sing it—without instrumental accompaniment—while whoever chose the song led the singing. It was amazing how everyone kept time, stayed in tune, and sang perfectly together. They even harmonized. It sounded incredible in that small room. Out the window, the snow was piled high around pine trees. To me, it seemed too bad that we were so far out in the woods and no other people could hear the singing. It was one of the most beautiful sounds I have ever heard.

After we sang, everyone quickly stood and knelled, facing their chair. I was expecting this, thanks to my research, and did the same as everyone else, but Mom remained seated, looking confused. No one seemed to notice or mind.

After prayer, Caleb gave the message. As you may have seen in Amish movies, usually Amish communities have a bishop. Because Unity is relatively new and small, the bishop travels between there and Smyrna, the Amish community in northern Maine.

He was not there that Sunday, and on the days he was not there they had one of the Amish men fill in as a speaker. That speaker was out of town, and I hadn't realized until then that Caleb would be filling in for that speaker.

Caleb led the service as the entire first chapter of Corinthians was read aloud by the men in the congregation. Each man took a turn reading.

The service was from 9:00 to 11:30 a.m. After, we ate a potluck lunch that all the women and girls set up. Caleb's family contributed the egg salad that I'd helped make. All the food was delicious. There were trays of sandwiches, meat pies, soups, casseroles, and plenty of baked goods.

After lunch, a young woman named Jolene talked to me for a while.

"So, what made you want to come here?" she asked.

"I want to write Amish novels and want to get to know the Amish so I can portray them accurately in my books. I want to see how you all live and experience it for myself. That way I can describe your lifestyle accurately in the books."

"That is great! I think not many writers do that. It's good that you are here to experience our lifestyle for yourself."

Again, relief and gratitude filled me.

"So what about you? Where do you live and what do you do?" I asked her, knowing she was clearly out of school.

"I live with Caleb's sister, Christina. I am the school teacher here," she told me.

I could tell she was not much older than me, and I was only twenty. "How old are you?"

She was twenty-two and had not gone to school beyond eighth grade, just like every other Amish student. My mother and I had the most education out of everyone in the community, and we had never even gone to college. We both had our cosmetology licenses, and I had a certificate in writing books, but no college degrees, and we still had the most education out of everyone there—even including the men.

After lunch, I met Caleb's sister, Christina, who invited me back to stay with her. I told her I would love to, and she gave me her phone number. She was lovely, and I hoped it would work out so I could come back to stay with her.

I talked to a woman about *rumspringa*, a time in a young Amish person's life when they are allowed to leave the community to try living outside the community.

"The Amish young adults in Unity do not do that because they all choose to remain Amish. It is a shock for them once they see the ways of the outside world. Sometimes they give in and become too involved with things like drugs and drinking. However, parents do not make their children remain Amish. It is up to the child. And most of them choose to stay. It is what they know," the woman told me. "Also, the Amish do not try to recruit people into joining. In fact, we discourage it. People who are not Amish—*Englishers*—may be able to live like us for a while, but then they give up because it is too hard. To be Amish, usually one has to be born Amish."

I, for one, could not live this way permanently. I would miss electricity, music, my laptop, my car and the fast-paced life I am used to. But the main character in my book *The Ring Thief* does leave the modern lifestyle for an Amish lifestyle. I think some people could do it, but it is definitely not for me. Our conversation did give me some ideas for the book. My main character in the book is a talented piano player. Would she be willing to give up her beloved instrument in order to join the Amish who do not allow instruments?

The events of the day flooded my brain with thoughts and information. After saying goodbye to everyone, we had to go home because of the snow storm. We made it home safely before the snow came down hard.

I couldn't help but wonder when I could return to Unity again. The Amish had made a lasting impression on me. I envied their community and lifestyle.

Tuesday, October 18th, 2011

I called Christina, Caleb's sister, a few weeks ago and she just called me back today. They had gone to Tennessee for two weeks, and she had lost my number. She said she was hoping I would call and leave my number.

Good news—Christina is willing to host me. I will be returning to Unity on the 22nd, and I get to stay until the 28th. I am SO excited!

Saturday, October 22nd, 2011

Finally, my car was packed and I was ready to leave, excited to return to Unity for an entire week. When I left my house today, I shut my dress in the door on the way out. It made me laugh. I am not used to wearing clothes like this.

On the way to Unity, I realized I didn't know which house was Christina's. I had never learned that detail. I knew she lived behind Caleb, but there were three houses behind him. I would have called, but I figured Christina wouldn't get my phone message in time anyway, because they didn't have a phone in their house. They used the community's phone. Oh, well. I'm sure someone will help me once I get there.

Around 9:30 p.m., I drove down the lane past Caleb's house, hoping my headlights didn't wake anyone up. Getting there that late concerned me. Maybe no one would be around to help, after all.

One of the houses behind Caleb's was still lit. I assumed that was Christina's home and drove up the dirt driveway.

(The photo below is of part of Christina's house.)

When Christina came out, holding her baby, Evangeline, and a battery-operated lantern, relief washed over me. It was her house after all.

(Above is Christina's house. Sorry it is so blurry. I took all these photos with an old cell phone.)

"Hi," she said. "Did you find our house okay?"

"Yes. I didn't know which house was yours, but I guessed this one was it when I saw the light on. I'm so sorry I'm arriving so late at night. I wanted to come earlier, but I got out of work later than I thought I would. I hope I'm not keeping you up too late."

"It's okay. Don't worry about it. Come on inside."

I gathered up my bags, and we went inside. Christina's husband, Edward, and Damaris, their three-year-old daughter, waited for us in the living room. Christina gave me a quick tour of the house and told me to make myself at home.

It is very similar to Caleb's house in terms of style and décor. Their house is two stories, and Edward's parents live in the basement. This is very common among the Amish. They take care of their elderly parents instead of sending them to nursing homes.

When you first walk into the house, there is a room where everyone hangs up their jackets and takes off their shoes. Then beyond that room is the kitchen, complete with a wood stove. To the left is a sunroom with huge glass windows and a porch with solar panels. To the right is a hallway with the bathroom and the stairs. The guest bedrooms are upstairs.

(Above is Christina's kitchen. Again, sorry it is blurry.)

Christina said breakfast was going to be at 7:00 a.m., then they all went to bed. I went upstairs and went to bed, too.

(Below is a photo of the room I stayed in with one of the battery-operated lanterns.)

Ashley's Amish Adventures: An Outsider Living with the Amish | Ashley Emma

Sunday, October 23rd, 2011

That Sunday morning, we walked a mile or two uphill and through the woods to get to church. Again, just like I thought last time when I was here, I'll never have an excuse to skip church again. When we got there, some of the women recognized me, like Rosie, who shook my hand.

Unlike last time, the church building was now finished. The room where church was held was large and had wooden floors and walls, and several installed windows. Next to this room is the school room, which was closed off. Downstairs was where everyone ate after the service. Though it had not been cold during the church last time, it was definitely warmer now. And now that I had already been to one of the church services here, I felt much more relaxed now that I knew what to expect.

As I waited for the service to begin, I counted about seventy-five people in the church, made up of thirteen families. Half of the service was in German, but it had a lot of English words thrown in, so I could keep up pretty well. Christina helped translate, whispering the sentences in English as the speaker spoke in German.

We sang several songs, but I couldn't find where we were on the page until we sang the last song. They were all in German and were sung very, very slowly. They were the slowest songs I'd ever heard! Still, they were very beautiful sounding like last time.

In the back of the room, they had a small mattress where the parents let their kids sleep through the two-and-a-half hour service. At one point there were six children on the mattress, all sound asleep facing different directions! They were all so well behaved.

I was happy when an elderly man, who I would later find out was Christina's father-in-law, started preaching in English. I could actually follow along, and his sermon was moving. It was actually quite similar to sermons I usually hear in church.

Church was from 9:00 to 11:30 a.m. When church was dismissed, more women came up to me and greeted me. A young woman named Lydia explained which children belonged to which families, and another girl named Ella Ruth invited me over to her house for the Singing that was later on. I accepted right away, since I missed out on the Singing last time because of the snow storm.

We went downstairs to eat lunch. The women set up lunch and made two large pots of coffee on a gas stove top. I talked with Regina and Cara, two girls I had stayed with in March, and then we ate lunch. The food was very similar to what we had last time.

I sat with Regina, Cara and some other girls. Most of the time they conversed in Pennsylvania Dutch, probably out of habit.

In the middle of the conversation, Regina said to the other girls in a hushed tone, "We should talk in English so Ashley understands."

"No, it's okay. I like to try to figure out what you're saying." Sometimes I could understand. I was recalling more and more German the more often I visited. The people here speak German half or most of the time, especially at home, but so many English words are thrown in that I can usually follow them. Damaris speaks German to me because she hasn't learned English yet, and now I can somewhat understand what she is saying. I know the words *spiele* (which means 'play' and is used frequently), *esse* (eat) and simple words like that which are said often. I wish I would have brought a German word book with me, but I am getting better. Maybe I learned German in school for a reason!

Despite my telling them it was okay to continue in German, to be polite, they continued in English. I'd have to practice more another time. But it was nice knowing exactly what was going on.

After everyone finished eating, the church sang the Lord's Prayer. All the girls then made an assembly line. By hand, we washed, dried, and put away the dishes of seventy-five or so people in about fifteen minutes.

I left with Ella Ruth to go get Caleb's daughters—who had already left—so we could go to the Singing. We walked back through the woods and talked about the dogs our families had.

We walked by a huge hole, and she told me it was an old manure pit they wanted to make into a pond for cutting ice to keep their food cold. That sounded really unsanitary to me, but I was too shy to say anything about it. They also plan to skate on it, and they go sledding down the huge hills in the winter.

We went to Caleb's, and I met a girl there named Sharon. She was very friendly and talkative. We were asked in advance to read a story or poem at the Singing, and I looked through my Bible for something. Regina, Sharon, Ella Ruth, and I took a pony wagon to Ella Ruth's house. A pony wagon is like a buggy, except it is open, with no roof.

Cars flew by and around us, and almost every driver waved politely. The girls talked with each other, and I leaned back on the pony wagon seat, thinking how content I was and hoping I could continue coming here after this week of research. I loved it here.

We arrived, and the horse walked right up to a post. One of the girls tied him to it, and then we went in the front room of the house. Everyone talked as Ella Ruth made popcorn in an old kettle on a gas stovetop.

When the popcorn was done, we sat around the large table in the kitchen. Ella Ruth put sour cream and onion flavored powder in the popcorn, and the popcorn was gone within minutes. I asked her if she had ever had popcorn with nutritional yeast in it. She said no, and some of the girls thought that was funny. It does sound weird, but it is actually really good.

Everyone got a song book that had mostly English songs, which I was happy about. First, we each went around the table and read a poem or story. When it was my turn, I explained that all I had with me was my Bible and I read Psalm 96, and they liked that one. Ella Ruth read a funny story about a princess who couldn't cry then finally could when she smelled an onion. Many more poems were read around the table, and when everyone was done reading, we began singing.

Instead of going shopping, going to the movies, watching TV or playing video games, this is the type of things the Amish teens in Unity do for fun. One of us would choose a song and say the song number aloud. Everyone would find the page, and the girl who picked the song had to start singing it alone, to start it out so everyone could join in on the same key. This happened at the beginning of every verse, and that was how they all started and ended on the same key without instruments. When it was my turn,

I lead all the other girls in singing "Take My Life and Let It Be." It was wonderful. They sang it beautifully.

After the Singing, Caleb's daughters brought me back to Christina's. Jolene's parents had arrived from Kentucky, along with her little brother, Anthony, and her sister, Sylvia. The family was very friendly and they engaged in many conversations with me. Jolene's parents had fourteen children! And I thought my family of six children was large.

Monday, October 24th, 2011

That morning, I wished I could take a picture of Damaris and Sylvia playing outside my window, because they were so adorable. I didn't because I would have felt bad about it, like I was invading their privacy.

Christina told me that all communities are different, but here they will not pose for pictures. A few times since I have been here I have wanted to take a picture of Amish people walking along the road, but I was afraid they would turn around and see me and not trust me anymore.

Christina said, "I don't mind if I'm driving down the road in my buggy and someone takes a picture of me, but I don't know how the others feel about it."

I decided to not take any photographs of them at all. However, they were fine with me taking pictures of objects like their houses, barns, and the scenery.

That morning, I went downstairs to help with breakfast. Jolene's mom introduced herself to me, saying she had never met an Ashley before. Ashley is such a common name, so that surprised me a little.

We had toast, eggs, cereal, and cookies I had brought. I'd never had cookies for breakfast in my life!

After we were done eating, Edward read from the book of Acts and we all knelt at our chairs to pray.

I did the dishes with Jolene's mom, who was very amiable. We hit it off right away. "We will be traveling all the way back to Kentucky by bus. That's how we got here. I just hope we don't have a long layover in New York City. But everything happens for a reason," she said.

She told me a story about how they were once in a buggy and Sylvia wanted a drink, but the motion of the buggy kept sloshing the drink onto her, so they stopped while she drank. Then another buggy and a car passed each other on the road ahead at the same time. She said she was sure that if they wouldn't have stopped, there wouldn't have been enough room on the road for the two buggies and car. They would have all passed each other at once, and there probably would have been an accident.

At 9:00 a.m. we started to make lunch. Christina sang while she worked. It seemed as though everyone sang here all the time, and they all sang well. They sang while doing things around the house, while walking down the road, and just for fun.

They don't have radios or music on their phones, but music is still a huge part of their lives.

While lunch was cooking, I picked two big boxes of grapes off their stems, cleaned them, and put them into jars for canning. Christina would eventually use them for juice and jam. At one point, there was a hornet in the box, which I almost accidentally grabbed along with a handful of grapes. That doesn't happen when you shop in a store, but the food isn't as fresh then, either.

While we worked, Christina told me about how she met her husband, Edward. They grew up together and courted for a year or so until they were married when she was twenty-four. She had had a few other proposals, but she declined them. When Edward proposed, she knew he was the one for her. People often ask me if the Amish marry very young or have arranged marriages, and in Unity, that is not the case at all.

"What is the average age when people get married here?" I asked.

"Usually between twenty and twenty-five, or it could be older. Most people think the Amish marry very young, but the marrying age is generally the same age as non-Amish people. Dating in the Amish community is strictly hands off—as in no physical contact of any kind until marriage, which even includes holding hands. Usually a courtship starts as 'dating,' where the couple may have a date once a month until they are engaged. When they are engaged, they can have a date once a week until they are married. Usually a couple does not date without serious intentions of marrying, and all Amish marriages last. There is no such thing as Amish divorce."

Jolene, the school teacher, was twenty-two and dating Christina's brother, Abner, who is twenty-five. Christina believed they would get married.

Another interesting fact is that when an Amish couple is married, they do not kiss at the altar because they believe it draws too much attention to them. After the ceremony, they have a big reception with lots of delicious Amish food. That part is similar to what I'm used to. However, our weddings are usually catered. The Amish do all the work themselves.

After a meal, all the men leave their dishes at the table exactly as they are, and they leave. They do not participate in meal preparation or clean up at all. Instead, while they are waiting, they read. The Amish read a lot, since they don't have TV. They read books just like us, as long as they are not immoral. However, I was flipping through a novel Christina recommended to me called *Tisha.* It was about a teacher in Alaska, and many of the words were crossed out. My guess was that they were profanity or words misusing God's name.

After we ate lunch, I washed the dishes while Christina pressure cooked and canned the grapes. I went to a deli down the road, bought two scoops of ice cream, plugged my phone into the wall, and waited there for an hour and a half while it charged. I found some nutritional yeast there and bought a container of it for Ella Ruth's popcorn so she could try it.

As I waited for my phone to charge, I wrote about my week. I hoped I could come back soon, and my mind began to wander. I decided to write my thoughts in my journal.

If Jolene marries Abner, I hope she invites me to the wedding. It is possible! I'd love to see an Amish wedding! When I get married I want to invite them to my wedding, but I wonder if they would come because it would be so different than the weddings they are used to, and it would be such a long car trip to pay a driver for.

As for dancing, I always thought they were against all types of dancing, but Christina said mostly they are against couple dancing, and it said in their song book that dancing is a sin.

I really want to go teach the children at school some fun dancing that each person does individually, and Christina said she thought that would be fine.

As I wrote, I looked at my hands. I had grape debris stuck under all my nails. There certainly was no need to paint fingernails here. The Amish women were always getting their hands dirty, and they were not afraid of it. A manicure would have been pointless.

As I sat in the deli and watched people come and go, I realized I was so used to seeing long dresses, white bonnet-type head coverings, and men in suspenders that people in modern-looking clothes now seemed odd to me. When I was in Unity, I felt a little self-conscious for not wearing a head covering. But they did not expect me to act just like them. Now I felt self-conscious for not wearing my modern wardrobe. Strange how I immersed myself into the community in such a short time. I still wondered if the Amish were aware of their clothing when they went to town and if they cared. I'd have to remember to ask about that.

A few times so far, Christina had had to remind me no one expected me to dress and act just like them. She had even told me again when we were at church. I had hung up my white jacket among the dozens of black coats hung on the wall.

"I guess I brought the wrong color jacket." I just wanted to blend in as much as possible.

She said, "Don't worry. We do not expect you to do everything like us!"

As I thought about my time in Unity and continued to write in my journal, I felt like we cooked and cleaned all day long. Every single meal was a big deal to the Amish. Each meal—with preparation, prayer and clean up—took us about two hours. Even breakfast was a big event. We made biscuits from scratch, cinnamon buns, pancakes...it was never boring.

I was so used to eating breakfasts that involve no cooking or cleaning. It saved so much time that way.

But the Amish believe mealtime should be bonding time. And maybe that is why they are so close. While I was there, I never saw any siblings argue. They all got along so well, like close friends. I never saw a child say or do anything disrespectful. It is not that they were all quiet and only spoke when they were spoken to.

They were lively and happy, but they knew how important respect was.

But don't they get tired of all the work and wonder why they can't use modern conveniences to get it done quicker? Then they would have more time for worship, prayer, fun, and family time.

I had only been here a few days, and I felt like I spent most of my time cooking and doing dishes. At home, it took me only a few minutes to load up the dishwasher. Here, dishes took up a huge chunk of each day.

It all came back to the issue of contentment Christina told me about. They were content with what they had and the way things were.

I wondered how long I could happily live that way.

Tuesday, October 25th, 2011

This morning we had pancakes with sausage gravy, which I thought was really different. Who needs maple syrup when you have gravy?

After breakfast, I asked Jolene if I could teach art and dance at school. I explained to her that it was not partner dancing, and she was happy to have me do it! She told me to show up at 1:30 p.m. on Friday, then she left with her family for Acadia National Park, which is a 47,000-acre recreation area in Maine.

Esther, a woman who lived down the road in the house where the Singing had been held, invited me to her house. I got picked up at 8:30 a.m. that morning by her, her son Tim, and her four-year-old daughter Debra. They were on their way back from dropping some of their other children off at school. I brought along my art supplies and the nutritional yeast I bought for Ella Ruth. We drove to their house on a pony wagon with a cider press in the back. We had to walk at the end because it was too much for the pony to pull along with our weight up a small hill. Once we got off the wagon, the pony was able to pull it to their house.

At their house, I taught Debra and her two-year-old brother Seth how to paint. We colored paper over leaves with pastels watercolors. They loved it! I was a private art tutor for a few years, so I knew a few fun art projects I could teach them.

Ella Ruth, Maria, and Esther cooked and helped me make mozzarella cheese from scratch. They put some ingredients with milk in a big pot which I cut, stirred, and strained.

I gave Ella Ruth the yeast I had bought and she said she would make popcorn later so we could try it.

Ella Ruth asked me, "Do you have TV?"

"Yes, but I don't have time to watch it much. I'm so busy all the time." It was true. I hardly ever watched TV.

The other boys in the family came in, and we had rice with beef and vegetables, bread, a cantaloupe I had brought, watermelon, cake, and milk.

They almost always had dessert, which was always something homemade, with lunch and supper. I guess they needed the calories and burn it off with all the hard work they did!

They put their dessert—usually a baked good such as cake or pie—in a bowl and pour milk over it. I have never seen this before, and I thought it would taste weird at first, but it is actually really good.

These are Esther's twelve children in order of oldest to youngest:

Caroline

Joseph

James

Timothy

Ella Ruth

Maria

Lily

Laura

Rosanna

Naomi

Debra

Seth

Their house reminded me of the movie *Cheaper by the Dozen*, but not as chaotic. Because there was no electricity, the children entertained themselves. They were happy doing simple things. They worked a lot doing chores and went to school (except for the small children), but they also knew how to have fun playing board games, jumping rope, singing, or running around outside.

Afterward, the boys read books while we girls cleaned up.

Esther said, "There are so many dishes with such a large family, but that's what we are here for. Right, girls?"

I faked a smile, wondering what she meant by that. I didn't think girls were made to just do dishes and housework, but maybe I had misunderstood what she had said. Maybe she had meant it was only part of what they were made to do—I wasn't sure.

We washed all the dishes and then went back to painting and drawing. I drew a horse and they loved it. I taught them how to make origami paper frogs and how to cut a paper a certain way that enables you to step through it.

They absolutely loved the paper frogs. We drew faces on them, and they enjoyed "feeding" each other's frogs by putting pieces of paper into the frogs' paper mouths.

The girls showed me the barn. It was huge! On the outside it looked like a huge greenhouse made of vinyl, and the roof was rounded instead of pointed.

They had cats, cows, horses, and enormous pigs. We went into a greenhouse where they stored peanuts and beans, and we shelled beans for a while and talked. I asked them questions, and they asked me questions, too.

"So what do you do for fun at home?" Maria asked me.

"My best friend and I get together a lot, and we like to go shopping or watch movies. We also dance together, so sometimes we choreograph new dance routines. I also write a lot, as you know, because that is my favorite thing to do. I also like to go out to eat with my friends and family."

"That sounds fun! Do you have a boyfriend?" Ella Ruth asked.

"No, not right now."

"What's your job like?" Maria asked. "Do you like it?"

"Well, I work at a busy salon. So I cut hair and color women's hair and do highlights. So I make their hair lighter or darker or put streaks in it. They call the salon and book appointments with me or sometimes I take people who walk in. But I also work at my mom's salon in her house. I like that a lot better because I make more money per service and I can work when I want to. One day I'm going to have my own salon in my house when I get married, I hope."

(Now I do have my own salon in my home.)

"Oh, wow! That would be so great to own your own business. Then you could be home with your children." Ella Ruth smiled.

"That's actually a big reason why I want to do it," I told her.

"Where did you go to high school? Did you go to college?" Ella Ruth asked.

"I was homeschool until high school and then I went to a small Christian high school. I didn't go to college, only hair school for one year."

Afterward, I went with Maria to sweep their bike shop.

(Below is a photo of their sign.)

Then Lily, Rosanna, Naomi, and Laura came home from school. We played jump rope for about an hour, then we played limbo and the high jump. I tied the ends of the rope together to make one big circle, and we held on to it and ran around. Little Seth laughed so hard, which made all of us laugh.

We went inside, and I taught the rest of the kids painting as we ate popcorn with the yeast I had bought for Ella Ruth. It was great to see them all having so much fun and learning. They loved learning new games, so I taught them how to play the "clothespin game." It is a game where each person gets five clothespins, and someone picks a word you are not supposed to say. We chose the word "what." When someone says that word, the person who catches them takes one of their clothespins. Whoever has the most at the end wins. We laughed so much the entire time.

"Mom, what do you want me to put in the lunches?" Lily asked as she packed lunches. All at once several of the girls said, "You said it!" and tried to take one of her clothespins.

They started to use the German word for "what."

I said, "What is the word for it?" and one of the girls took one of my clothespins. We decided no one could say "what" in German either.

To trick the girls, I said, "Whoopie pie," and, "Walk," and "Won." Soon Esther started playing too. Sometimes the girls would say something quietly or mumble something to make another say, "What?" It was so hard to not say it! Even the older boys, who were usually very quiet and never spoke a word to me, laughed. Soon their father Irvin came home from work and asked what we were playing, smiling at our silliness.

Then we played a game called Evolution, which is much like Pictionary, except the pictures change from one thing to the next depending on your teammate guessing on what the picture is. I drew a moose that ended up being a chicken. The children laughed the entire time.

They showed me their rooms, and I told them about the books I've written. They were very interested in reading one of my other books, *Identity*, so maybe I'll send them a copy one day when it is published.

Wednesday, October 26th, 2011

The next morning, I awoke to a strange *tap tap tap* noise that ended with a *ding*.

That has to be a typewriter.

I woke up and looked around the guest room. It seems to me that almost every Amish home has at least one guest room. That interested me, given how large their families are. But I'm assuming it's because they are so hospitable and welcoming. And for that, I was grateful.

(Below is a picture of one of the bedrooms in Esther's house.)

The clacking and ringing continued, and I wandered downstairs to investigate. There sat Irvin at a desk, typing away.

"Good morning," he said.

"Good morning. What can I do to help?"

"You can mix this grape juice." Esther handed me a jar of purple liquid. "Mix it with a jar of water." Then she gave me a jar of Stevia, a non-sugar natural sweetener they love, and told me to put in one tablespoon. I mixed it for a few minutes as Debra climbed onto the counter and watched me. We poured it into cups as we waited for the biscuits to finish.

The younger children made even more paper frogs while waiting for breakfast. This time they taped strips of paper inside for tongues, which they found to be very silly. I had to agree.

Then we had morning devotions, which Irvin led. We read Matthew 6, which talks of how to pray and teaches the Lord's Prayer, and each person took turns reading a verse. Afterward, Irvin went around asking us what we thought of the passage.

My answer was, "Sometimes the good things you do in secret make more difference than the things done in the open."

He agreed, and the discussion continued. Then we went over the Lord's Prayer, and the oldest boy didn't know what "hallowed" meant.

"It means holy," I said quietly.

"What was that?" Irvin asked me.

"It means holy," I said, "Or separate, or sacred."

He looked slightly surprised that I knew this, but I didn't take offense. They didn't know everything about my culture just like I didn't know everything about theirs. Then Irvin asked the boy what the first part of the Lord's Prayer meant to him and what he thought, but the boy said he didn't know. To me, it means when we pray, we should acknowledge the holiness of God, just like in the first line of the Prayer. But I didn't say anything. Irvin talked with the boy about it for a moment, then we kneeled at our chairs to pray before we ate breakfast.

After breakfast, it was 7:45 a.m. and almost time to go. As the girls hitched up the pony, Esther asked me, "Is it very different here than what you expected?"

"The first time I came it was. When I first arrived in Unity, I had no idea what to expect. I didn't know you could have running water without electricity." I also thought they had outhouses, but I left that out. I chose only to mention a convenience or two, leaving out our feelings and beliefs. It still stuck with me that the girls thought they were born only for menial labor and nothing more, but I had no desire to get into a philosophical debate, particularly one that they might find offensive.

"Do you cut your hair?" She motioned to my long braid. "Or is it against your religion?"

"No, it's not against my religion to cut it. I just like long hair because I can do a lot of different hairstyles with it. I've had long hair most of my life, actually."

When it was time for the girls to leave for school and drop me off at Christina's, I thanked Esther, and she invited me back to do laundry with them tomorrow, which is a day-long event that I couldn't wait to experience. I climbed into the pony wagon with Rosanna, Laura, Naomi, and Lily—she drove the wagon and was twelve years old—and we took off with Maria on her bike beside us. Maria thought it was funny that I thought she was eighteen or nineteen when she was actually fourteen. They all just seem so much older and mature for their ages.

They taught me the spelling of their last name, which is very German-sounding. It took me a few tries to say and spell it correctly. As we passed by on the wagon, people waved politely. Esther said they usually do. That simple gesture fascinated me. At home, people bustle about and barely acknowledge each other on the street. Of course, I don't know my whole community the way the Amish do, so that could have something to do with it. On the other hand, I have a feeling the Amish would be that friendly with strangers, too.

We went over all the siblings' ages and birthdays. Lily and Laura actually knew all the names and birthdays in their family, except for only a few birthdays. I told them I hardly know all of my siblings' ages and birthdays, and I have only five siblings.

"Do you want to see pictures of my family?"

"Yes," they all said.

"The pictures are on my phone. Is that okay?" I asked.

"Sure!" They all agreed. It surprised me that they are fine with looking at or using other people's phones, but they cannot own one of their own.

They loved the pictures of my twin sisters.

"Wow! They look so alike! And they look like you," Lily said.

I showed them pictures of my house, my whole family, and my friends. They liked to see what my home looked like. "Your house is so nice!"

By the time I showed them all my pictures, we were at Edward and Christina's house.

"We're so glad you came over. We had a lot of fun!" Lily said.

"I'll try to come tomorrow to help you with laundry. I hope I can. Thanks so much for having me over!"

"You're welcome. Bye!" Maria waved and rode away on her bike.

"Bye!" the other girls called.

I waved and went into Christina's house, and they drove their wagon down the lane.

Later that day, we drove to Christina's brother Andrew's house and stayed from 11:00 a.m. to 3:00 p.m., where a group gathered to make applesauce. Maria and Sharon were there, and I helped them pick apples to put in a huge container.

Andrew's family grew and picked the apples themselves. We washed them, cut them up, and boiled them. We didn't have to peel them, for which I was grateful. I helped Sharon put all the boiled apples into a device that was secured to a table. Hot juice splashed us occasionally as the juice dropped into a bucket as I guided it in with a spatula.

The apples were strained by the device and the peelings came out one side while the applesauce emptied into a bowl. While the liquid was still hot, they canned it. We made one hundred quarts of applesauce that afternoon for several families to share all year.

While we worked, the younger children busied themselves by looking at books and playing with homemade play dough. I read them a few stories. Again, even though several of them didn't know English yet, they seemed to understand. They nodded and giggled when I read the funny parts, and they pointed to the pictures. We read one of my favorites, *Frog and Toad,* which is the first chapter book I ever read on my own when I was little.

I went back to helping with the apples. As Sharon and I strained the boiled fruit, she told me about her five brothers, including a little redheaded boy named Charles who entertained himself by pushing chairs around as we worked.

As the days pass, I am continually impressed by how well the children treat their siblings and parents and how well behaved they all are. I got the feeling I wouldn't witness any tantrums here.

As we continued to strain the apples, there was some commotion by the window near the porch. We gathered around the window to see what everyone was laughing at. Andrew's white turkeys jumped up on the porch and started pecking away at the buckets of apples. Sharon went out and scared them away, and we all giggled at her flapping her arms and yelling at them. The women cut off the bitten parts of the apples and used the rest for sauce.

Afterward, Christina, Damaris, Evangeline, and I drove to an old museum with Jolene, her brother Anthony, her sister Sylvia, and her parents. The yard was full of old stoves!

The front room of the museum did not look like a regular museum. When we first walked through the door it looked like the inside of a house. There were newspaper articles on the walls about the museum and its owner, Joe.

(Below is the sign on the museum.)

We went into a large room with dozens of old stoves and a huge collection of goofy salt and pepper shakers.

Then we found a massive room with a high ceiling that was filled to the top with hundreds of toys. We noticed a switch on the wall that said "activate toys." When we flipped it, all of the toys came to life. Music that sounded like a marching band blared as everything moved, twirled, or danced. There were dolls, puppets, trains, cars, and marionettes. Wooden planes with whirling propellers hung from the ceiling.

(Below is a photo of the room full of toys.)

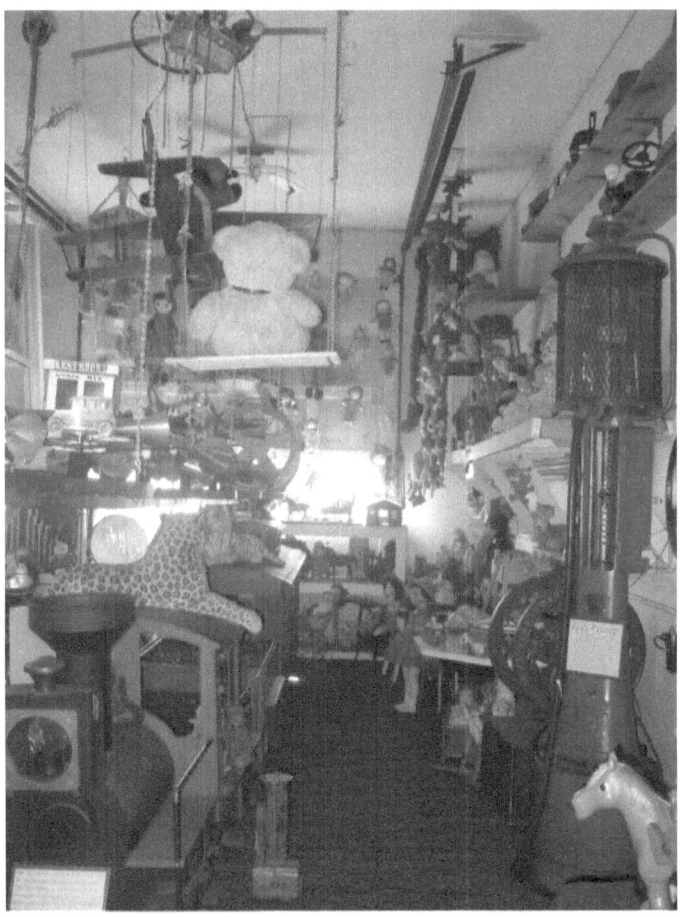

We walked around the entire room, fascinated at the colorful and complex arrangements.

There was a bright red wooden train complete with a whistle. We laughed at the silly ostrich marionettes marching around in a circle—they were as tall as Damaris! We leaned over the side of a fenced-in area containing mini cars that zoomed around a racetrack, and I wondered who had made this amazing room.

Joe showed us all the old pianos, stoves—one was made sixteen years before Lincoln was president—cars, and other antique things.

There were rows and rows of player pianos. I sat down and began playing. (I took piano lessons for ten years.) We sang "God Bless America" and "Let It Snow," but Christina, Jolene, and her parents had never heard those songs before.

Joe said, "Sing with us anyway. Oh wait... Can you even read the lyrics?"

I looked at him, somewhat flabbergasted. Did he really think the Amish didn't know how to read?

My Amish friends remained unflustered. Christina simply said, "Yes, we read." I didn't understand how she wasn't offended. She just smiled at the man while I stared at him with wide eyes, shocked at both of them. Did non-Amish people often assume things like this about them, and the Amish were just used to it?

"Don't you only go to school a few years?" he asked.

I couldn't believe that a man who lived just down the road from several Amish families knew so little about them. Yes, maybe many people know the Amish only go to school until eighth grade. But eighth graders can read!

Amish people are not uneducated or illiterate. In fact, they speak, write, and read English more correctly than most people I know. Our society has grown so used to slang and incorrect English that we don't even realize we speak with incorrect grammar anymore. Sometimes, when someone does say something that is correct English, it sounds strange to us. For example, it should be "This is she" instead of "This is her," or "as I said" instead of "like I said."

"We go to school until eighth grade, but we all read and write well," Christina explained, voicing my thoughts.

"Oh, I'm sorry," Joe apologized. "I jumped to conclusions."

"It's okay. We don't expect people to know everything about the Amish way of life," Christina explained graciously.

We sang "The Old Rugged Cross" and my Amish friends knew that one.

Joe had a car used in the movie *Skylark*, the sequel to *Sarah Plain and Tall*, which is a movie I grew up watching. He assumed I was Amish, even after I told him I had seen the movie several times. He must not have realized that the Amish do not watch movies or TV.

He said, "Do you ladies have a ride home?"

"Yes," I said, "we have my car."

"You have a car?" His eyes widened and he chuckled.

I showed him my car keys. "Yes. I'm not Amish."

"You're not? But you are dressed like them."

"I'm just visiting them. I'm not wearing a head covering, and remember how earlier I said I had seen the movie?"

"Yes..." he said, still confused.

"Amish don't have TV!" I smiled. I thought the fact that Amish don't have TV was common knowledge. Apparently not.

Later, I helped Christina with dinner by slicing up some pears she had grown. Then she sent me downstairs in Edward's mother's part of the house to watch the milk on the stove and make sure it wouldn't boil. We were going to make hot chocolate. While the milk heated, I talked to Edward's mother about the museum and the things we saw there.

"The owner assumed that the Amish do not know how to read. Do people say things like that to you often?" I asked.

"Sometimes. *Englishers* sometimes assume things about us that are not true at all. But we are not bothered by it. Some people think we have arranged marriages, that we are a cult, or are not educated at all. I'm glad you are here putting in the effort to learn about our ways."

I smiled, amazed at her and Christina's attitude toward the situation.

The stove gave off a surprising amount of heat that filled the entire house. They didn't even need another source of heat.

The children knew to stay away from the stove, except Evangeline, who toddled a little too close to it sometimes. It sure was hot when I stood near it. It had been hot in the kitchen we made applesauce in yesterday, too, even though all the windows had been opened in the house.

I brought the milk up when it was ready, and we mixed in some store-bought hot chocolate mix. They do not make everything from scratch like many people think. They also buy products like cereal, toothpaste, crackers.

At dinner it was only me, Christina, Edward, Damaris, and Evangeline, so we had an unusually simple meal. We had the pears, the pineapple I had brought, and popcorn for supper. Edward left right after we ate because he had a phone appointment in the shanty to call his brother.

Christina asked me to play with the girls while she cleaned up. I taught Damaris how to paint while Evangeline sat in my lap. We painted a cat, a horse, and an overflowing bathtub. She was actually very good for her age. Again, all she said to me was *Ja*, but in Pennsylvania Dutch and German the J is pronounced like a Y.

Me: Do you want to paint?

Damaris*: Ja.*

Me: Do you want to paint a horse?

Damaris: *Ja.*

Me: What color?

Silence.

Me: How about blue?

Damaris: *Ja.*

All our conversations were like this—short and to the point, but we managed to communicate with each other pretty well without anyone translating for us.

Later on Jolene and her family returned. They looked at my self-published book *Identity* that I had printed myself, and they thought it was great. Anthony was especially interested and asked if he could borrow it for the night, so I let him.

That night, as we all headed to our rooms for bed, I realized I had finally stopped habitually feeling around on the walls in the dark for light switches. I was getting used to having no electricity.

Thursday, October 27th, 2011

The next morning, Jolene's father, Mr. Baker, read the devotions. Anthony gave me back my book, saying he liked it. He had stayed up all night and read the whole thing!

However, he said the part about the time traveling was unrealistic. Of course time travel is unrealistic. That's the fun part about fiction! Sometimes it is very unrealistic. He also told me the way the main character thinks is a lot like how he thinks sometimes. Overall, he had obviously thought it was interesting enough to read in one night.

Jolene's mother, Mrs. Baker, did the dishes with me and told me how much she enjoyed getting to know me. She gave me their address so I can write to them. We got their luggage together and brought it out the door.

The Baker's driver arrived. The Amish commonly hire locals to drive them to where they need to go, like the bus station. A middle-aged woman in jeans came into the house and sat down at the table. I realized I was not the only non-Amish person who knew this family well as they started chatting. Edward's mother gave the driver a drink.

She introduced herself to me and then asked me all about who I was and why I was there. She told me she frequently drives the Amish who live around here. Later on, an Amish family told me she does it in exchange only for some home-cooked Amish food instead of money. That's how good their food is!

The Bakers said goodbye to me, and Mrs. Baker gave me a big hug. "It makes me sad when I get to know someone and then realize I will probably never see them again. May God guide us both, for eternity is so long."

I wiped away a tear as they walked out the door. I was moved by her words and hated to see her leave.

We loaded up the driver's truck, and the Bakers set off on their two- or three-day journey back to Kentucky.

Afterward, Christina took me outside to see the ice house.

It is located on the side of the house behind a removable door. It is probably the size of my kitchen or larger, is made out of cement, and has a high ceiling.

"In the summer it has more ice in it, but this is what we have for now," she told me. The floor was almost covered in large blocks of ice that were about one or two feet long and one or two feet high.

We went back inside and I played with Damaris and Evangeline while Christina cleaned. As I played with the children, I talked to Edward's mom about my book *Identity*. She said she had read some of it. She also liked the *Chronicles of Narnia*, Tolstoy, *Lord of the Rings,* and the book Christina's father Elmo had written called *Give Me This Mountain.*

She told of a story in the book about a boy who received a nice new buggy that he loved, but then he purposely damages it. Halfway through, when the boy smashed the buggy's lights and slashed the seats, the author said that is how youths treat their bodies by drinking, doing drugs, and not practicing abstinence. It was a fascinating premise.

I told her about the Amish books that got me interested in learning about the Amish and coming to Unity. I then asked about bikes, because one book described the bishop banning bikes in an Amish community, but in Unity it was allowed.

"See?" she said. "Not all Amish are the same."

I told her in movies the head coverings are different looking. I saw a movie called *The Shunning,* set in Lancaster County. She showed me a book called *Just Like Mama*, also set in Lancaster. Edward's mother liked the pictures because they are accurate. She told me the head coverings in Lancaster are more heart-shaped, the women twist their hair on the sides, and they wear pink dresses.

The head coverings here are simpler. The backs have a round shape and there are eight pleats on each side. It is so interesting to me how each community in different in their styles of clothing, the way they speak, and their rules.

I read Damaris and Evangeline a few books until we sat down to eat. Christina made a casserole—they make a lot of those, and they are all so good—layered with moose meat and pork on the bottom, salsa, sour cream, cheese, and then a biscuit layer on the top. It was one of my favorite things I had there. And there was applesauce—not the applesauce I had helped make—and cinnamon buns.

After we finished, I left to go to the store to get more dish soap and some fruit for Christina. She wanted to make a fruit pizza.

Then I drove to Ella Ruth's house, but I could see right away from all the clothes on the clothesline that they had finished with the laundry already. I went in anyway and sat on the couch with Esther, Seth, and Debra as Esther looked at a magazine with them and talked in German about the pictures. I learned new words by seeing her point to the pictures and say what was in them. Between what people have taught me and by listening, I can somewhat converse and say simple phrases, especially with the children who only speak German/Pennsylvania Dutch. I can tell the kids to come eat or ask them what something is.

As we looked at the magazine, I helped Debra string Cheerios for Seth to eat. Esther said all her kids liked to do that at one point. I've never heard of it, but it was fun. It reminded me of stringing popcorn for Christmas trees.

I went outside with Maria, Laura and Debra to the greenhouse. We picked peanuts off plants for an hour or two and played the clothespin game. We chose the words "that" and "the." That was hard! We said those words all the time and didn't even realize it.

I took pictures of the peanuts they grew and picked themselves. There were four big shelves full of them. We had two buckets full of peanuts at the end. To me, that did not seem like much from all those plants, but they told me that it was a good amount.

After, I helped in the kitchen by making apple dumplings. The girls peeled apples and ate some of the peelings.

I said, "If you like the peelings, then why do you peel the apples?"

"They taste so much better in the dumplings when the apples are peeled," Laura said.

After I took a bite of the apple dumplings I said, "You're right! It would not be as good with the peelings on."

This is a similar recipe to what we used. Of course, we had to double it to feed the large family.

Ingredients:

2 cups of flour

A teaspoon of cinnamon

A half cup of apple juice

One cup of diced apples

One tablespoon of cornstarch

Two 46 ounce cans of apple juice

Directions:

In a medium bowl, mix the flour, cinnamon, and one half cup of apple juice. Stir until smooth. Mix in apples. Pour all apple juice unto a pot with a tight lid and bring to boil over medium heat. Mix in diced apples, cover pot and let it boil for twenty minutes. It is important to not remove the lid during this time. After the twenty minutes are up, remove the dumplings from the pan and set aside. Stir cornstarch into remaining apple juice in the pot and cook until it is thick. Serve over dumplings.

Makes 8 servings. May serve immediately (plain, with milk, or with ice cream) or allow to cool.

(We ate ours with milk on it, of course.)

As I swept the remaining apple peelings off the floor and washed dishes, Esther asked me if I had a dishwasher.

I said, "Yes, but sometimes it doesn't work well. I'm used to doing dishes by hand."

She said it was refreshing to see a young person who is not Amish willing to work. I just liked to help.

"I get the impression from what people say that young adult *Englishers* can sometimes be disrespectful or lazy. Do you think that is true?" she asked.

"Well, all the teens I know are very respectful and are good workers. But I bet there are many teens who are not like that."

"Well, I do not know many teens who are not Amish, so I wouldn't know."

I knew she wasn't trying to insult our culture. I just hoped I was setting a good example.

As we washed dishes from baking, I ended up accidentally spraying myself with the sink hose. Rosanna giggled with me at my clumsiness.

For dinner, we had a really good stew Ella Ruth made with chicken, vegetables, gravy, and stuffing. There was also white cabbage coleslaw that looked like grated cheese. Then we had the apple dumplings, and they were delicious.

As we cleaned up the dishes from dinner, a rubber band fight started. They ducked and ran and fired bands at each other, running around the house, laughing hysterically the whole time. This was the first time I had seen the children make a lot of noise.

Lily asked me above the chaos, "Does it get this crazy at your house?"

"Sometimes. But we don't have quite as many people at my house. Sometimes when we have friends over it gets this loud."

She said with a laugh, "We have so many people here, we don't need to have friends over to have fun!"

Once the "fight" died down, we drew pictures and painted at the table. I drew the profiles of Lily, Ella Ruth, Maria, Rosanna, and Naomi. The children were amazed at how some of the pictures closely resembled them.

Friday, October 28th, 2011

This morning we ate breakfast and I did the dishes again. Christina told me she was going to do laundry, and I was so excited to help her because I had missed out on helping the family of twelve the day before.

Washing clothes took a long time! They used an old-fashioned Maytag washer run by gas that swished the clothes back and forth, and then they put it through a wringer that squeezed most of the water out. We rinsed it in a bucket and sent it through the wringer again, then hung out on the clothesline. I was afraid my fingers would get caught in the wringer, which could have happened if I was not careful.

(Below is a photo of the washer we used.)

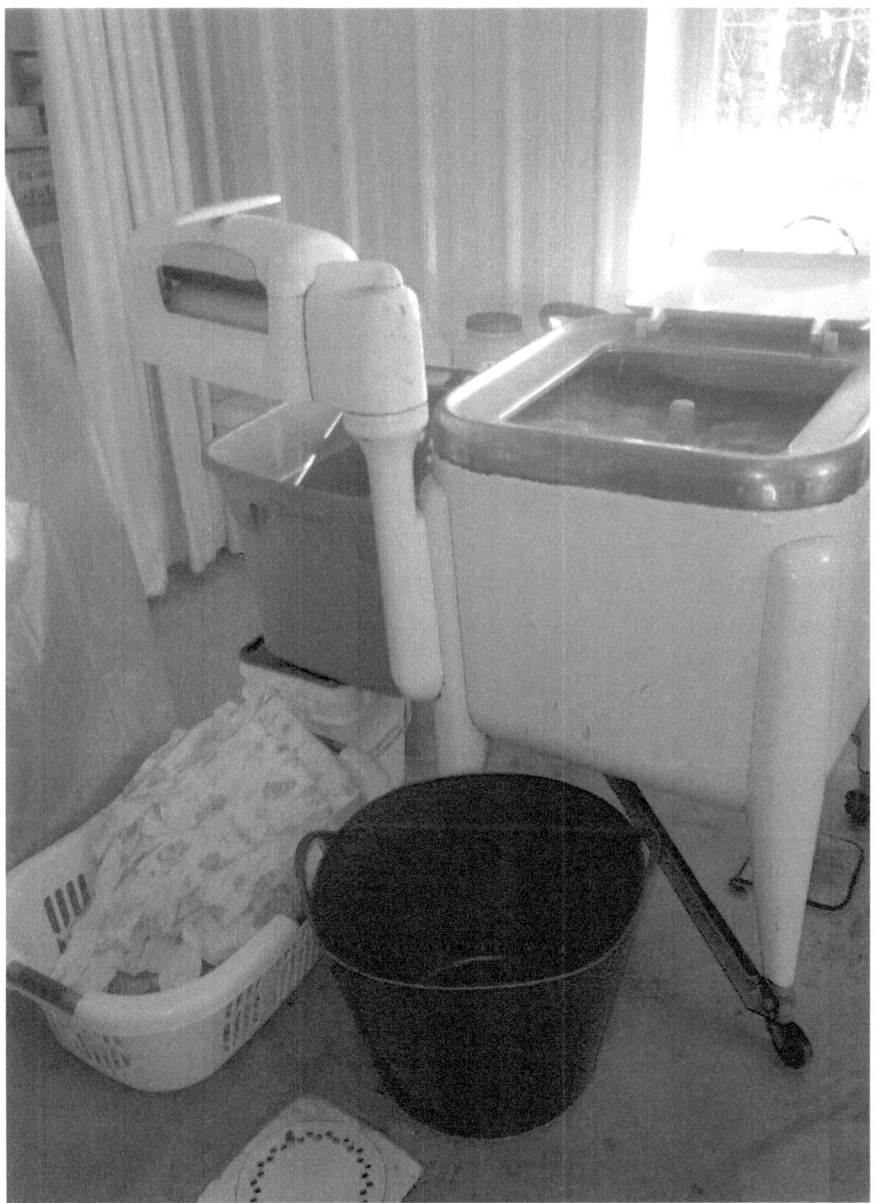

After my stay with the Amish, a few people told me stories of people they knew that got their arms caught in it. There is a button to push that opens the contraption if that does happen, but I didn't want to find out what that would be like!

After the laundry was done and hung on the clothesline, I packed up everything to bring out to my car so I would be ready to go. As I walked out the door to bring my duffle bag to the car, Damaris saw me with my bags and she started to cry.

"I'm not leaving yet," I told her. "I'll be right back."

Christina held her and comforted her. She looked at me with a smile and said, "She'll be okay in a minute. She's grown attached to you."

I had really bonded with the little girl over the week, even though she was rather shy and we speak different languages. I had read to her whenever she brought a book to me, and I had played with her and Evangeline while Christina was busy. Now I felt sad to get to know her so well only to leave her, but I knew I would come back here soon.

I went back to the museum and took dozens of pictures of all the stoves and the room full of toys, and I found Joe puttering around in his wheelchair. I asked him if he would take a picture with me and he asked one of his workers to take it, telling me he was somewhat camera shy.

After we took the picture, he told me he was going to Florida for the winter, but the museum would stay open all year long. He said he hoped to see me there again someday, and I told him that was very possible.

Next, I drove to Lydia's house for lunch. She and her big dog came out to greet me. Her sister Tabitha and her mother Katie were inside. They own a bakery where they bake from 5:00 a.m. to12:00 p.m. every Thursday and Friday to sell their goods at a market on Saturday.

(Below is their house.)

Their bakery is open all week though, I think. It is located in a building right next to their house. They make whole wheat breads, pies, rolls, turnovers, and the like. They have an oven with multiple doors and compartments where they bake several things at once.

When I got there, I helped them make blueberry turnovers. It was a time consuming process. There were lots of dirty dishes to wash.

Lydia's father and brother came in. We sat down and had the silent prayer. He asked me about myself, and somehow the dinner conversation turned to Noah's Ark. I told them about a church sign I saw once that said, "Where did Noah put the woodpeckers?" They thought that was pretty funny, as I had when I had first seen it.

For lunch we had noodles they had made from scratch along with salad and bread that had also been made from scratch. I would have enjoyed helping make the noodles and bread, but I hadn't been there to assist them.

After lunch, I had to leave right away to make it to the schoolhouse in time, but not before I bought three turnovers and four pecan rolls to bring home to my family. I arrived at the school at 1:20 p.m., just in time to teach at 1:30 p.m.

When I walked through the doorway of the classroom, all the children looked at me but didn't make a peep. Jolene had me sit on the side of the room while they did spelling.

The school room looked like any other classroom, except for the clothing the students wore, of course. The walls were decorated with colorful art work, and there were posters and a big chalkboard. Jolene had her own desk, and each student had a desk like the ones in modern public schools. There were about twenty-three children in the class.

They do not take time off for holidays, but they do for an occasional wedding. Their summer break starts in April and ends in September. Without holidays, they get things done faster, and they are all extremely well behaved in class, so maybe at eighth grade they are very much ahead of their eighth grade public school counterparts.

The Amish only go to school until eighth grade because they believe further education is prideful. The children are also needed at home to work, because chores take longer with many kids and animals and no electricity. People might say the lack of electricity robs the children of a proper education, but all the Amish families I have met own successful businesses and are content with their level of schooling. Quite frankly, they are content with everything.

Irvin owns a windmill company and his boys have a bike shop where they sell bikes and do repairs. Lydia's dad makes furniture, and her family owns a bakery. Caleb has a store, and he and Edward sell their produce.

For them, high school is unnecessary. They don't need to make a lot of money and the women seem happy to stay home and work and take care of the children.

It's like what Christina was saying about contentment. They are content with simple lives and they seem as happy, or even happier than any other people I know. Their families are close and they stay together. They respect each other and all get along.

For them life is about faith, family, food, work, and fun.

I saw first-hand their love of family, so I had no doubts about that. But I wondered about their faith. Did some of them just follow the customs because that's all they knew? Or because they were expected to. Or for fear of being shunned? Or did they really believe the tenets of their faith? Did they just hope they'll go to heaven, or did they fervently believe their lifestyle would get them there? I wondered if they suffered crises of faith like people of other religions sometimes do.

Their faith certainly did seem genuine—each and every one of them. I supposed it had to be to live in such a way.

One of the things that interested me the most about their faith was that they didn't evangelize. But I remember the Amish woman from church telling me that most Amish are born into it. Very few outsiders join the Amish and fewer end up staying.

Perhaps that's why they didn't evangelize. No point in trying to get someone to join your faith if you don't expect them to be able to last in it. I don't, however, think they are completely against evangelism, because Christina asked me if I evangelized at work. I hoped I showed them not all non-Amish were the same. I hoped I was a good example of non-Amish Christians.

Jolene finished up spelling with the class and then introduced me to them. Next was recess. I told them whoever wanted to could come with me and I would teach them exercises and stretching outside.

Most of the girls joined me while the boys were a little more hesitant. We did some simple stretching and jumping. The girls stood in front of me while the boys watched sheepishly off to the side. I told them to start off by doing jumping jacks, but not one of them knew how to do it. I couldn't believe it!

We did twisted and jumped and touched our toes, and they laughed the whole time, saying it was silly and funny, probably feeling self-conscious. I even had them hop around in a circle on one foot, and they laughed even harder. Then they surprised me by asking me to teach them a dance. So I taught them parts of the hip hop and jazz dances I was learning that year. They did quite well learning them, and they laughed at the dancing, too.

After we went inside, I taught all the children how to make paper frogs. Many of the children asked me to draw faces on them. After all the frogs were done and everyone was dismissed, I asked Jolene how she kept the class so quiet.

"They just know they are not supposed to talk until they are called on," she said simply, like it was obvious.

"Well, what if they do?"

"I suppose they would get in trouble, but it never happens. They are taught at home to not talk in class until they are called on."

"I wish I could get my dance students to be that quiet in my class," I told her, laughing.

On my way out, a few of the children asked me to go to their houses, but I told them I had to go home, but I would come back in the winter or spring. They thanked me for teaching them, and I got in my car.

Back at Christina's house, she asked me how teaching went and I told her how they laughed at the ballet dancing, and she asked me to show it to her. She thought it was quite interesting. She had probably never seen anything like that before.

I wrote down my address for them and hugged Christina and Evangeline goodbye. I knew I would miss them. I thanked Christina over and over for having me, and she told me I was welcome back.

Before I left, Christina gave me a copy of a book that her father Elmo wrote before he died—*Give Me This Mountain: A Selection of Views and Values*. It is a collection of short stories. He had written stories and articles for a magazine and collected them all to compile into a book. His book was written on a typewriter, and his mother said he typed out several versions of it before it was published. They probably have a limited number of copies, so the book was a precious gift. What she wrote in it was even more precious:

To my friend Ashley,

I've enjoyed spending time with you this week. I pray God will supply your every need and bless you!

Love, Christina and family.

During my visit to Unity I realized how much I respect the Amish.

People think they are quaint, but they know so much about the world, and living their lives is hard work. It takes so long just for them to go somewhere nearby.

I love the freedom of owning a car. I was happy to drive around after not driving for a few days. However, my week there had been so fun. I had the best time with them, and I felt so blessed to have experienced something so incredible.

I think I could live like them for a few weeks or even a few months, and then I would miss my phone, car, and laptop. I wouldn't like to do my writing with a typewriter like Elmo did. I would really miss my laptop. Even if it is a hunk of junk.

However, I barely noticed not having electric lights after a few days, and since the house is heated by the wood stove, the only electronic household appliance I think I'd really miss is a microwave, fridge, and outlets to charge things with.

I am really becoming more thankful for the life I have. There is so much work the Amish have to do. To me, I have much more time to serve God living the way I do without having to spend extra hours doing chores the long way, and I am content with the life I have. However, living with the Amish has made me want to become closer to God, and I am planning on doing just that. It is something that does not happen overnight—it takes work, prayer, and studying the Bible. The Amish certainly know a lot about that.

I went to Unity to do research and learn about the Amish, but really I have learned a lot about myself, and I have made good friends there. I know the Amish of Unity see me as a friend, because they have told me I am welcome to come back any time.

I decided to leave the copy of *Identity* behind so my friends in Unity could read it and pass it on. I wrote an inscription in it before I left.

To my friends in Unity:

Thank you for a fun learning experience. I learned more than I thought I would... Not just about facts, but about your kindness and love and friendship, and about God and myself. I will always remember this week and be grateful for it.

Love,

Ashley.

Letters to and from the Amish

(Some are abridged to leave out personal information.)

10.7.11

Dear Christina and Edward and family,

Thank you so much for letting me stay with you. It was one of the best weeks of my life, and I did not want to go back home! That transition back into my fast-paced life was a little strange at first, and I miss the quietness and peace of Unity. Everyone here was eager to hear about and learn about my stay with the Amish. They were fascinated, and some even said they would like to go for a week. They were impressed that I went a whole week without power. When I got home, there was a snowstorm, and many people lost electricity and were very disconcerted. Some people went a few days without power, and when I said I just went a week without it, they couldn't believe it! It's hard to go a few days without it for some people when they have lived their whole lives using it every day, I guess.

In my week in Unity, I realized life is so much more than electricity and clothes and money. These are just things we don't need. I learned that life is about worshipping God through loving people, working hard, and having fun. I wish life was that simple here where I live. Sometimes I think I can see a glimpse of it when people help each other or sing in church.

Anyway, I plan to come back between February and April of next year! I wish you all a safe winter. It is still very warm here, and sometimes it feels like spring even though we had a snowstorm recently. I hope it will be a mild winter for everyone.

I am looking forward to my next visit with you very much. I have been reading the book your father wrote, Christina, <u>Give Me This Mountain</u>. My mom is reading it, too, and we enjoy it very much.

I will bring/mail you a copy of the book I am writing about my week with you. It is almost finished!

Again, thank you so much for the memorable week and your friendship.

-Ashley

P.S. What process would one go through to join your Amish community? I was just wondering. Thanks!

October 16th, 2011

Dear Baker family,

I very much enjoyed getting to know your family during my stay with Christina and Edward. How was your trip back to Kentucky? I prayed for a safe journey for you. How long did it take to get there by bus? Did you have any layovers?

I appreciate Anthony taking the time to read my book, Identity. I left it behind for whoever else wants to read it.

Going to the museum with you was very fun! I also enjoyed getting to know Jolene. She let me go to school that Friday and teach the children art and outdoor activities at recess. They are very good learners! Jolene really does a good job at keeping the class in order. It is the most well behaved class I have ever seen. She is a very good teacher.

Thank you for a fun week. It was fun learning from each other. And thank you for your friendship!

-Ashley

October 7th, 2011

Dear Esther and Irvin and family,

I had so much fun with all of you! My mom was so impressed that I made cheese! I had so much fun playing with all you girls and teaching you art at your house. It was also very fun to go to your school. You are all very good learners.

I miss Unity very much. Sometimes when I drive around Biddeford and Kennebunk, I see fields with barns and pretend I am in Unity for a minute.

Thank you so much for inviting me into your home. I had so much fun, and I laughed more than I have in a long time! Whenever I see a clothespin, I will think of you girls.

I left a copy of Identity with Christina for anyone who wants to read it. I will also mail/bring you a copy of my book I wrote about my week in Unity. It is almost done.

Again, thanks so much for an unforgettable week. I hope to see you all again soon!

-Ashley

(On the back of this letter I drew a cat that looked like the cat we drew when we played Evolution. I also drew some of the paper frogs we made.)

November 2011

Dear Friend Ashley,

Greetings in love of Jesus' name. How are you and your family? Thank you for your letter. Yes, we had a safe journey home, much to be thankful for.

We didn't see snow in Maine, but I had wished to see some on the evergreens there. I love evergreens. But when we got to Boston, it started snowing and then in Pennsylvania it turned out we got 7 or 8 inches. So that was different for October, not even Halloween.

We are building a new house. The blocks are being laid, but now it is rainy today, and it's supposed to rain tomorrow—so it's on hold.

Our son, Raymond, shot a big buck, a 10-pointer. It is 220 pounds. So we had bologna made and it is good.

Yes, we want to appreciate our schools a lot, for it is so worthwhile. Our son, Lincoln, is not in a plain church, but his girlfriend Tanya is an art teacher and she cannot make her pupils do a thing. She may not even lay her hands on them to restrain them from hurting the others. She is teaching at a different school this year, as she has gotten convictions to wear a head covering and this school is so much better. But she still longs over the poor little children that she used to teach—those who are being drawn into evil through their parents.

Tomorrow we plan to shop at a place called "Habitat for Humanity." It's a thrift shop for builders. When one builds a house, there are so many small and large things to buy. It is interesting. We have built 2 houses before—one in Pennsylvania and one in Montana.

So have you found anything edifying in your visit in Unity? Would you consider living that lifestyle? It really isn't so hard. We have it pretty good compared with poor folks in many other countries. We likely don't do enough to help them. But we will sometimes do some volunteer work for CAM if there are disasters close by like tornados, floods, etc.

Our sons enjoy helping.

Well, I will close. I wanted you to know that I will remember you and I care about you—it was interesting to meet you.

May God guide us both, for eternity is so long...

Love, Mrs. Baker

December 2011

Dear Mrs. Baker,

It has been very busy around here! I am getting my wisdom teeth extracted on February 6. Do the Amish also have surgeries like that and/or go to the doctor for check-ups?

I am so glad to hear you got home safely. What a warm winter we have had here so far until very recently! In fact, sometimes I check the weather in California and it has been ten degrees warmer here in December.

Congratulations to your son Raymond on his buck! I don't know much about deer, but his deer sounds impressive to me. My dad also got a deer. He saw it early one morning in the back yard while he was drinking his coffee. He ran outside in his pajamas with his gun and shot it from our porch! It is a funny story we love to tell. He didn't even have to go in the woods. My mom made a very good stew out of it.

I have heard of "Habitat for Humanity" but I never really knew what it was. How amazing that you built 2 houses before and God supplied all the material. How is the building coming along?

I really loved going to Unity and I will hopefully return in February or March. I really do miss it there, and I actually did consider what it would be like to join the Amish church. I think I could do it, but I don't think it is meant for me. I heard many Amish people say you usually have to be born Amish to be Amish. I don't mind all the work (it's not much different than at home except for the laundry part) and I love the church and prayers and community. I believe mostly the same things the Amish believe. Everyone is very friendly and the families are close. They all get along so well. That is a precious thing. I miss the peacefulness there. Life is so fast-paced here, sometimes I wish it would all slow down. Time seemed to stand still in Unity.

I love God with my whole heart, but I believe I am called to serve where I live. Lately I have been working in the church nursery and teaching Sunday School for the children. I also lead in the young adult ministry, which I love.

You are very right when you say you have it better than many people. There certainly was no shortage of food as far as I could tell! And it was all so delicious. I sponsor and send money to a girl in Uganda named Emily. She bought one fourth of an acre of a banana plantation with the $75 I sent her!

If I lived an Amish life, I know I would definitely miss my family. I would miss my car, a microwave, and my cellular phone. Also, writing books would be so much more difficult for me to do without my computer, and I have always known I am meant to write books.

I found it all so interesting in Unity, and so have so many people back here at home. Dozens of people have bought my book so far. It is called Ashley's Amish Adventures. They all are amazed with the story of my stay in Unity and all the things that happened. I sold almost all the copies I had, but I will order some more and send one to you and your family!

Thank you so much for your letter. You are the first and the only one to respond so far. (I sent out one to Christina and Edward and one to Esther and Irvin.)

It was so wonderful to get to know you and everyone in Unity. May God keep you all safe this winter!

Love,

Ashley

December 31, 2011

Dear friend Ashley,

It's so hard to believe this is the last day of the year. It's thirty degrees and raining so there's some ice, but hopefully it will keep warming up so road conditions won't get too bad. It's a perfect day to just stay home by the woodstove and listen to the sound of the rain pattering on the roof. I'm so glad for the cheery sunroom with lots of windows on a day like this. The sky is gray with a mist/fog hanging low over the soggy landscape.

I'm hoping and praying for safe traveling for the vanload heading to Ontario today. Caleb, Cara, Beth, Joanna, Jonas, my mother, and Simon (my cousin) are the ones who went. They plan to be gone for almost a week.

Thank you for the nice letter we received a while back. I apologize for not responding sooner. December was so busy, sometimes it seemed hard to keep up. I had very little spare time for letter writing. We also enjoyed your visit here, and I thank you again for being so cheery and helpful with the food you brought. I'm glad you found your time here worthwhile.

I guess you're probably also enjoying the mild weather this winter where you live. We have had some snow and a few storms, but overall it hasn't seemed like much of a real winter yet. But there is still time for that before spring comes. I'm glad to have winter shortened a little. ☺

Damaris and Evangeline both have colds, which I'm really hoping they'll get over soon. It's hard to keep a child's nose clean when it is so runny. ☹ Besides, a cold can make one feel downright miserable, especially a stuffy head cold where one's sinuses make you feel like you're suffocating.

I'm becoming quite interested in growing herbs to make my own home remedies for my family. I wish I had more for this winter's colds and flus, but I have been giving the girls some grape juice with Echinacea mixed in and some elderberry and honey syrup that I think helped relieve their colds somewhat.

Two weeks ago we traveled to Smyrna for a four-day visit to help a family with a butchering project. Edward and his brother and some others killed, gutted, scalded, and scraped 12 hogs and 1 cow for about a half dozen households. Then we cut up some of those to make sausage, hams, bacon, and steaks, and the fat was rendered for lard. The bones were cooked in a big kettle, then scrapple was made with the broth, meat scraps, organ meat, corn meal, flour, and seasonings. I wonder if you know what scrapple is. I wasn't used to eating it before I got married, but I've learned to like it quite well. We eat it for breakfast with eggs, maple syrup, or apple butter.

I hardly know where to begin to answer your question about the process required to join an Amish community. In one way it is just as simple as going to a community and saying, "Here I am. I want to be a part of your community. I am here to learn and help." But on the other hand, if I would try to define all the adjustments a person goes through in the process of "pulling out of society" and blending into a plain community, it could sound pretty complicated. Of course, the biggest requirement in actually becoming part of a group is sharing the same faith and values. Faith in God and Jesus and a dedication to taking the Bible very seriously and being willing to let it order your life is a must.

I'm really looking forward to reading your latest book.☺ I'm curious whether you took your visit here as the basis then wrote a novel with fictitious characters or if you did it like a diary or what approach you took to your "Amish Story."

You probably remember that Caleb's wife Rosie and Irvin's wife Esther are sisters. A few weeks ago they received the unexpected news that their father, who lived in Indiana, passed away. So Irvin's family and Caleb's family and other relatives from here and in Smyrna were gone for several days over the time of his funeral. I took Regina's place as teacher at the school for two days while she was absent. I enjoyed the chance to teach again, but two days was long enough. I was glad to get back to being a stay-at-home wife and mother. Edward's mom and my mom helped Edward with caring for the girls so they didn't really mind my being gone much, but I still wouldn't want to do it often. I can't imagine having to leave them at a daycare center like a lot of mothers do in society.

Well, I'll close with wishing you a healthy, happy winter.

Love,

Christina, Edward, Damaris, and Evangeline

January 30th, 2012

Dear Christina, Edward, Damaris, and Evangeline,

This winter has been surprisingly warm! We have had a few storms, but it is not nearly as bad as some of the winters we have had before.

I hope you are all in good health. The flu and cold have been circulating through my home and at work, but thankfully I have not gotten sick yet.

I think the butchering project you mentioned in your letter was very interesting! That is a lot of meat! We get a side of beef from the farmer down the road who hays our fields. We also get raw milk from him. We still have moose meat from my dad's moose, and with that we make moose burgers and moose chili.

About the book… Tonight or tomorrow I will order some more copies. They have sold so quickly! I will bring them to you when I visit again in spring 2012.

I did not realize Rosie and Esther are sisters. I am so sorry to hear about their father. It is always so hard to lose a family member. But it is good to take comfort in knowing they are in the Lord's hands.

Were you a teacher before you were married? I didn't know that! When was that and how long did you teach? How wonderful that you got to do it again. What an excellent group of scholars those children are!

Well, I close praying for your health for the rest of the winter. Mrs. Baker and I have exchanged letters, and I sent one to Esther and Irvin's family. Tell them I said hi if you see them. I miss you all, and I will see you again soon!

God bless!

-Ashley

p.s. I have never heard of scrapple!

(On the back of the letter I drew a squirrel who eats near my house.)

***

Thank you so much for reading about my adventures!

Note from the author: I hope you enjoyed this story.

I would appreciate an honest review for this book because reviews are actually very important. They help other customers know more about my books. Your opinion matters!

Thank you! Please feel free to email me at ashley@ashleyemmaauthor.com. I'd love to talk with you!

Don't forget to visit http://www.AshleyEmmaAuthor.com/to download free Amish books!

Looking for something new to read? Check out Ashley's other books!

Other books by Ashley Emma on Amazon

Coming 2019:

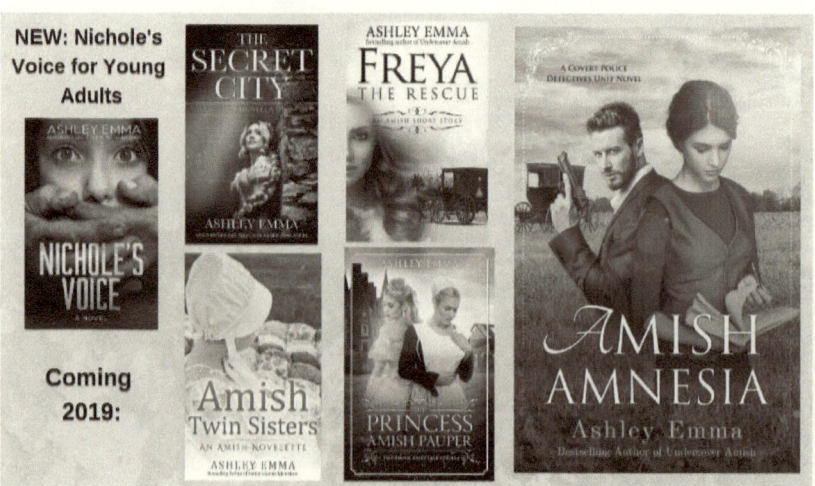

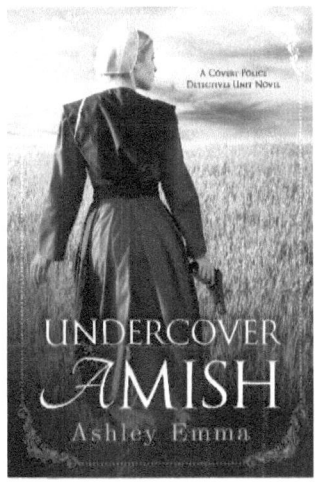

UNDERCOVER AMISH

(This series can be read out of order or as standalone novels.)

Detective Olivia Mast would rather run through gunfire than return to her former Amish community in Unity, Maine, where she killed her abusive husband in self-defense.

Olivia covertly investigates a murder there while protecting the man she dated as a teen: Isaac Troyer, a potential target.

When Olivia tells Isaac she is a detective, will he be willing to break Amish rules to help her arrest the killer?

Undercover Amish was a finalist in Maine Romance Writers Strut Your Stuff Competition 2015 where it received 26 out of 27 points and has 455+ Amazon reviews!

Buy here: https://www.amazon.com/Undercover-Amish-Covert-Police-Detectives-ebook/dp/B01L6JE49G

NOW AVAILABLE! AMISH UNDER FIRE

After Maria Mast's abusive ex-boyfriend is arrested for being involved in sex trafficking and modern-day slavery, she thinks that she and her son Carter can safely return to her Amish community.

But the danger has only just begun.

Someone begins stalking her, and they want blood and revenge.

Agent Derek Turner of Covert Police Detectives Unit is assigned as her bodyguard and goes with her to her Amish community in Unity, Maine.

Maria's secretive eyes, painful past, and cautious demeanor intrigue him.

As the human trafficking ring begins to target the Amish community, Derek wonders if the distraction of her will cost him his career...and Maria's life. Buy here: http://a.co/fT6D7sM

Free eBook!

FREYA: AN AMISH SHORT STORY (Book 1 in the Freya Series)

After Freya Wilson accidentally hits an Amish man with her car in a storm, will she have the courage to tell his family the truth—especially after she meets his handsome brother?

Get it free: https://www.amazon.com/Freya-Amish-Short-Ashley-Emma-ebook/dp/B01MSP03UX

New release! FREYA: THE CONFESSION (Book 2 in the Freya Series)

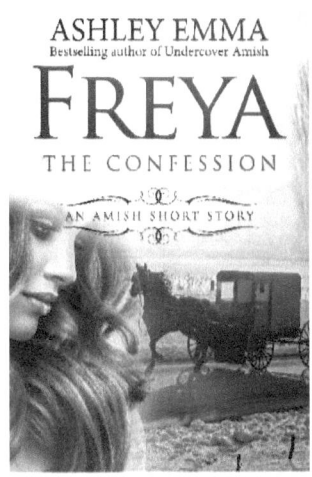

Adam Lapp expected the woman who killed his brother accidentally with her car to be heartless and cruel. He never expected her to a timid, kind, and beautiful woman who is running for her life from a controlling ex who wants her dead.

When Freya Wilson asks him to take her to his family so she can tell them the truth, he agrees.

Will she find hope in the ashes, or just more darkness and sorrow?

https://www.amazon.com/Freya-Confession-Amish-Short-Forgiveness-ebook/dp/B076PQF5FS

ASHLEY'S AMISH ADVENTURES: AN OUTSIDER LIVING WITH THE AMISH

Ever wondered what it would be like to live in an Amish community? Now you can find out in this true story for young adults and middle grade readers.

https://www.amazon.com/Ashleys-Amish-Adventures-Outsider-community-ebook/dp/B01N5714WE

FEARLESS AUTHOR: PREPARE, PUBLISH, AND LAUNCH YOUR OWN EBOOK

Have you always dreamed of becoming an author?

"...The list of places to promote your book along with the step-by-step publishing and marketing checklist is well worth the cost of this eBook."

---Nicole Cruz, www.nicolecruzproofreader.com

In *Fearless Author*, I will show you how I launched my own bestselling books.

https://www.amazon.com/Fearless-Author-step-step-self-publishing-ebook/dp/B06XJGRRT1

Excerpt from Undercover Amish

Chapter One

"Did you find everything you were looking for?" Jake asked.

Olivia Sullivan looked up to see her husband staring at her with furrowed brows and narrowed eyes. The anger flickering in them would soon grow into a hungry flame. He wouldn't yell at her here in the grocery store, but she should hurry to avoid a lecture later at home.

For a moment, she pondered his question. Had she found everything she was looking for?

No.

This was not the life she had signed up for when she had made her vows to Jake Sullivan.

"Olivia? Did you hear me?" His voice, low and menacing, came through clenched teeth.

"Sorry. I just need to find some toothpaste. I'll be right back."

"Hurry up. I'm hungry and want to go home."

Liv scurried with her basket toward the other end of the store, her long purple dress flapping on her legs. She tugged on the thin ribbons of her white prayer *kapp* to make sure it wasn't crooked and almost ran in to her neighbor, Isaac Troyer.

She halted so fast, her basket tipped and her groceries clattered to the floor. "Hi, Isaac. I'm so sorry! I almost ran you over."

"It's all right, Liv. Don't worry about it!" He grinned, green eyes sparkling reassuringly. Then the smile slid from his face and concern shadowed his expression.

Fear swelled within her. Did he know?

She squirmed and avoided his gaze. "I'm so clumsy. I really should watch where I'm going." She shook her head, clearing her thoughts as she dropped to the floor to pick up her groceries. Isaac hurried to help her.

"Really, everyone does these things. So how are you, Liv?" he asked in all seriousness, using the nickname he used to call her when they had dated as teens. They had been so in love back then—until Jake came along and stole her heart with his cheap lies. Isaac was an old friend now and nothing more. The piece of her she had given to him when they had dated died the day she married Jake.

She told herself to act normal, even if he did suspect something.

"I'm well. How are you?" She reached for a fallen box of cereal. Her purple sleeve rode up her arm, revealing a dark bruise. She took in a quick, sharp breath and yanked her sleeve down, turning away in shame.

Had he seen it?

Isaac rested his fingers on her arm. "Liv, be honest. Is Jake hurting you? Or did you 'walk into a door' again? You know I don't believe that nonsense. I've known Jake since we were children, and I know how angry he can get. And I know you might be silly sometimes, but you aren't that clumsy."

She sure wasn't silly anymore. Her silliness had also died the day she married Jake.

Olivia stared at Isaac wide-eyed, unable to breathe. He *did* know the truth about Jake. Her pulse quickened as the grocery store seemed to shrink around her, closing her in. Who else knew?

"You don't deserve this, Liv."

What would Jake do to her if he found out Isaac knew?

"Isaac...promise me you won't say anything. If you do, he will hurt me terribly. Maybe even—"

"Olivia! Are you okay?" Jake strode over to them. He helped her up in what seemed like a loving way, and no one else noticed his clenching grip on her arm.

Except Isaac. His eyes grew cold as his jaw tightened.

He knew.

Oh, God, please don't let him say anything.

No one would believe him even if he did. Jake was known for being a polite, helpful person. He was the kind of man who would help anyone at any time, even in the middle of the night or in a storm. No one would ever suspect him of hitting his wife.

He hid that side of himself skillfully, with his mask of deceptive charm that had made her fall in love with him so quickly.

Jake finished piling the groceries into the basket as Isaac stood.

"Good to see you, Isaac." Jake nodded to his former childhood friend.

"Likewise. Take care." Isaac offered a big smile as though nothing had happened.

When Liv glanced over her shoulder at him as she and Jake walked away, Isaac stared back at her, concern lining every feature of his face.

Most of the buggy ride home was nerve-wracking silence. They passed the green fields of summertime in Unity, Maine. Horses and cows grazed in the sunlight and Amish children played in the front yards. Normally she would have enjoyed watching them, but Olivia squeezed her eyes shut. She mentally braced herself for whatever storm raged in Jake's mind that he would soon unleash onto her.

"Want to tell me what happened back there?"

Jake's voice was not loud, but she could tell by his tone that he was infuriated. Who knew what awaited her at home?

"I bumped into Isaac and spilled my groceries. He was just

helping me pick them up," she answered in a cool, calm voice. She clasped her hands together in her lap to stop them from shaking, acting as though everything was fine. Their buggy jostled along the side of the road as cars passed.

Did he know what had really happened?

"I was watching from a distance. I saw him touch your arm. I saw the way he smiled at you. And I saw the way you stared at him. You never look at me like that."

Here we go. She sucked in a deep breath, preparing for battle. At least he hadn't heard what Isaac had asked her. Jake was always accusing her of being interested in other men, but it was never true. He was paranoid and insecure.

"You know I love you, Jake."

"I know. But did you ever truly let go of Isaac before you married me? Does part of you still miss him?"

"No, of course not! You have all my love."

"Then why don't you act like it?" His knuckles turned white as he clenched his fists tighter around the reins. "Why don't you ever look at me like that?"

How could he expect her to shower him with love? She tried, but it was so hard to endure his rampages and live up to his impossible standards. Yes, she had married him and would stay true to her vows. She would remain by his side as his wife until death.

However soon that may be. Every time he had one of his

rampages she feared for her life more and more.

She had given up on romance a long time ago. Now she just tried to survive.

If only her parents were still alive… but they had been killed along with the rest of her family in a fire when she had been a teenager. How many times had Liv wished that she could confide in her mother about Jake? She would have known what to do.

"I'm sorry, Jake. I'll try to do better." She told him what he wanted to hear.

"Good." Smugness covered his face as he glanced at her and sat up a bit taller.

When they arrived home, he helped her unload the groceries without saying a word. She knew what was coming. He internalized all his anger, and one small thing would send him over the edge once they were behind closed doors.

When everything was put away, he stalked off to the living room to wait as she prepared dinner. She began chopping vegetables, and not even ten minutes had passed when he stomped into the kitchen. As he startled her, the knife fell on the counter top.

Jake snarled through clenched teeth, crossing the room in three long strides. "You love him, don't you?"

"No, Jake! I told you I don't love him. I love you." She struggled to keep her voice steady. They had had this fight more than once.

"Are you secretly seeing each other?"

She spun around to face him. "No! I would never do that." She might wonder sometimes what her life would have been like if she had married Isaac, but that didn't mean she loved him or had feelings for him, and it certainly didn't mean she would have an affair with him. Happy or not, she was a married Amish woman and would never be unfaithful to her husband.

"I can see it all over your face. It's true. You are seeing him." He lunged toward her, pinning her against the counter top.

She tried to shield her face with her hands. The familiar feeling of overwhelming panic filled her. Her heart pounded as she anticipated what was coming. "No, that's not true!"

"After everything I've given you!" His eyes burned with an angry fire stronger than she had ever seen before. He raised his clenched fist and swung.

Pain exploded in her skull. Her head snapped back from the impact. Before she could recover, he wrapped his hands around her neck, squeezing harder and harder until her feet lifted off the floor.

She clawed at his hands, but he only clenched tighter. Her lungs and throat burned, her body screamed for oxygen.

This was it. She was going to die. She was sure of it.

A strange calm settled over her, and her eyes fluttered shut. It was better this way.

Her eyes snapped open.

No. Not today. For the first time in her life, she had to fight back.

She tried to punch him, but it was as if he didn't feel a thing. She tried to scream for help, but her vocal chords were being crushed. She reached behind her for anything to hit him in the head with. Her fingers fumbled with something sharp, and it cut her hand. But she ignored the pain.

The knife.

She gripped the handle. Before she could reconsider, she thrust the knife as hard as she could into the side of his neck.

Blood spurted from the wound as his grip loosened. His eyes widened in shock, and his knees gave out as he crumpled to the floor.

"What have I done?" She inhaled shaky breaths, struggling to get air back into her lungs. Tears stung her eyes. Bile crept up her throat, and she clamped a hand over her mouth. Panic and fear washed over her and settled in her gut.

She had stabbed her own husband.

A sob shook her chest. "Oh, dear Lord! Please be with me."

There was so much blood. Her stomach churned and her ears rang. Her head was weightless, and her vision tunneled into blackness. She slid against the handmade wooden cabinets to sit on the floor.

She should run to the phone shanty and call an ambulance, but she couldn't move. There was no way she could run or even walk all the way to the shanty without passing out. She would have gone next door to her aunt and uncle's house, but they were out of town.

As her vision tunneled, she wasn't sure if she was possibly losing consciousness or dying from being choked.

Either way, she was free.

Chapter Two

Six years later

"Jefferson! Run the other way!" Olivia shouted as she sprinted around the side of a broken-down house in Augusta, Maine. Her partner, Officer Jefferson Martin, bolted around the opposite side of the house, hoping to catch the culprit, who had just run to the other side. Maybe they could meet him in the middle and the criminal would be trapped in the fenced-in yard.

When Olivia thought of the young girl this man had kidnapped, she pushed herself even faster, her hair flying behind her. She reached the corner of the house, lifted her pistol, and swept the area. The perpetrator swung a rusty crowbar at her head. She ducked just in time to dodge it.

It thudded into the house right beside her face. She whipped around and shoved him up against the wall. "Nice try."

He struggled in her grasp, but she held onto him tightly as her partner rounded the corner and helped hold him down. When the perp would not stop wriggling and shouting protests, Jefferson pinned him to the ground and handcuffed him. "George Burke, you are under arrest for kidnapping. You have the right to remain silent…"

Jefferson finished reciting Burke's rights to him as he led him to the police car and shut the criminal inside. Jefferson questioned him about where the girl was, but the man said nothing.

"You think the girl is in there?" Olivia asked her partner,

nodding toward the shabby house.

"Maybe, since he bolted out the back door when we pulled in the driveway. Let's go check it out."

A second patrol car arrived as backup and guarded the criminal while Olivia and Jefferson entered the house, weapons drawn.

"Not exactly a home fit for being in an interior decorating magazine." Olivia wrinkled her nose at the piles of dirty dishes in the kitchen, the messy floors, the questionable smells. In the laundry room, baskets of clothes covered the top of the washing machine. She held up her Military and Police Shield pistol as she poked her head around the corner. "Clear!"

"Clear in the living room!" Jefferson called.

"Let's check the basement."

They approached the door, and he quickly pulled it open. "Anybody down there? Police!"

No response. The partners glanced at each other, nodded, and descended the stairs, looking carefully for any sign of life or movement.

They poked around for about ten minutes, looking for some clue where they could find Miranda Nelson, the little girl Burke had kidnapped. They had evidence he had taken her, but they didn't know where he was keeping her.

"Hey, wasn't there a washing machine upstairs?" Olivia raised an eyebrow at the beat-up appliance placed crookedly against a wall.

"Yeah, there was."

"This one is just taking up space. I know this guy isn't very tidy, but why have two washing machines, especially when one looks like that? This might be nothing, but I have a weird feeling about it." Liv walked over to it and looked behind it. "There's something back here."

Jefferson hurried over and helped her move it aside to reveal a small door in the floor. Olivia reached down and flung it open. "Miranda? We're the police. Are you down there?" She reached for the flashlight on her belt.

A soft whimper sounded in the darkness. While Jefferson called the paramedics, Olivia aimed the beam of the flashlight in the hole in the floor, which revealed a space a little bigger than a small closet. There, illuminated by the light, sat a young girl with her hands tied and her mouth covered with duct tape.

Anger flooded Liv's veins. How could a person do this to a little girl? She had been missing for days. Who knew how long she had been down here? If only Olivia could get her hands on that guy…but she wouldn't. Besides, the other inmates in prison would show him how people felt toward criminals who kidnapped little children.

"Miranda, my name is Detective Olivia Mast, and I'm from a unit called Covert Police Detectives Unit. May I come down? This is my partner, Officer Jefferson Martin, and we are going to take you home."

The girl looked up at them for a moment with tired eyes, then slowly nodded.

Olivia climbed down, and Jefferson followed.

The girl began to make sounds, as if she was protesting. She couldn't speak with that tape over her mouth. What was she trying to tell them?

"Jefferson, go back up. I think she is afraid of men right now," Liv told him quietly.

"You go ahead." He climbed up and took a few steps away.

Olivia bent down and crawled to the girl in the small space. "I'm going to take those ropes off, okay? I'm going to cut them, but I'll be very careful."

The child calmed down and let Olivia saw through the knots with her pocket knife. "I'm going to take off the tape now."

After Liv pulled off the tape, Miranda winced but quickly recovered. "Are you really taking me home?" Her eyes grew big, hopeful.

"Yes, Miranda. Your family is waiting to see you. They missed you so much." Liv offered her hand. The girl's small hand held on, and Liv pulled her up. The child wobbled and fell into Liv's arms.

"My foot hurts. I can't walk." Miranda pointed to her ankle. Olivia wasn't sure if it was a sprain or not, but paramedics would be waiting outside soon.

"May I carry you, Miranda?" Olivia asked the girl.

Miranda nodded and reached up towards her. Olivia scooped

her up and went back upstairs with Jefferson, who made sure the way was clear before them.

When they stepped outside, Miranda covered her eyes to shield them from the bright light. She probably hadn't seen the sun for several days. Olivia handed her to the paramedics so they could examine her.

"Stay here with me, Olivia." Miranda's voice sounded soft but desperate.

"Okay. I will."

"You did it again, Liv."

Liv turned to see Jefferson smiling at her. Her partner was a few years older than she was, around thirty, and handsome. She knew he liked her, but Olivia wanted to keep things professional. Besides, she was too devoted to her career to have time for a boyfriend.

"I'm impressed with how you found those clues that led us to the kidnapper. How did you know about the washing machine? And how did you know she didn't want me to come with you when you got her out?"

"If I were a little girl kidnapped by a man, I think I'd be afraid of men I don't know. Even a police officer."

"Well, it's a good thing we have female police officers, especially you. Victims trust you more, and you have a way with kids." He smiled at her again. "When you talk to kids, you're actually nice to them."

"What are you saying?" She playfully hit his arm. Liv didn't trust anyone, and she liked to be upfront with people, even if it wasn't polite. She was not the same meek and quiet woman who had left the Amish.

"You're not always as sweet as sugar, that's all." He gave her a nod. "I still can't believe you cut all your hair off. It looks great."

She tried not to blush as she reached up for the ends of her hair. "Thank you." She had recently cut her long, dark brown locks and now had a bob haircut with bangs. It had caramel highlights and was longer in the front, since the hairdresser had said that was in style. Liv hadn't really cared. She had just wanted it shorter.

Liv had grown up with long hair and had never been allowed to cut it. For a few years after she left her Amish community, it was hard for her to let go of. But finally she decided she needed a change, and she liked it. It was much better than the long French braid she had always worn it in, which always got in the way when she worked.

It had been her last tie to her Amish roots. She had even changed her last name from Sullivan back to her maiden name, Mast. Now that she didn't look Amish at all anymore, she could fully move on. Well, except for her Amish dress and prayer *kapp* in a box on the top shelf of her closet. She'd never be able to part with them because her mother had sewn them for her.

"So I hear you've got some vacation time saved up. You going to go anywhere?" Jefferson asked.

"I was thinking somewhere without snow. Maybe the Bahamas."

"You deserve it, Liv."

She didn't know about that, but she sure couldn't wait to get out of Maine for a while, away from all the heinous things she saw every day. She imagined a sparkling ocean with soft sand between her toes. And no one shooting at her.

Some commotion drew her attention, and she turned to see Miranda's father, Mr. Nelson, approaching and asking lots of questions. Olivia and Jefferson walked toward him.

"Hi, I'm Officer Jefferson Martin from Covert Police Detectives Unit. Detective Mast and I found your daughter today." Jefferson extended his hand.

"I just got to see Miranda, but I wanted to quickly thank the team for finding her. Where is this Detective Mast? I'd like to thank him personally." Mr. Nelson shook Jefferson's hand.

She cleared her throat. "I'm Detective Mast, sir." She stuck out her hand.

Mr. Nelson ignored her hand and stuck his hands in his pockets. "Oh. You're a detective? Really?" He gave her a once over.

Olivia tamped down her annoyance and crossed her arms. This was not the first time she had seen someone react like this. "Yes."

"She's the one who coaxed Miranda out of the house. Miranda wouldn't come near me. It's a good thing we have great detectives like Liv." Jefferson gave her a proud smile. That was one thing she loved about him. He always had her back in any situation. "In fact, Detective Mast found most of the clues today that led us to your daughter. She was the one who discovered where she was being kept, in a secret room under a washing machine."

"Is that so?" Mr. Nelson looked her over again. "You don't really look like a cop. You're too pretty to be a detective." He flashed her a smile, and Jefferson raised one eyebrow. She wanted to roll her eyes.

Ugh.

"Well, nice to meet you. I need to go check on Miranda." She spun on her heel and marched back toward the medical team. The girl tugged on her sleeve and stared at her, even smiling a little.

"I prayed God would send an angel to rescue me," she said in a soft voice.

Olivia couldn't help but chuckle. "I'm no angel, kid."

"But God did send you. Thank you for coming to get me," she replied as the paramedic inspected her ankle.

"You're welcome, Miranda."

Liv hadn't prayed in six years, and she didn't plan on doing so anytime soon.

She had left God behind the day she had left the Amish.

*

"Olivia, come see me in my office." Captain Branson took a swig of his coffee and nodded his balding head toward his office door at Covert Police Detectives Unit headquarters in Portland, Maine.

Bodyguards, police officers, special agents, and detectives all worked together in this building and in the field. Liv loved this place.

"In a minute. I'm just—"

"Now, Liv!" he shouted and disappeared into the office.

With a sigh, she closed the vacation website on her laptop and put the gorgeous images of the Bahamas out of her mind. She finally got a minute to herself at her desk, and *now* Branson wanted to talk. She picked herself up and stepped into his office, wondering what she had done wrong. Had she forgotten to label evidence or wipe out the microwave in the break room? Or was it the prank she played on Jefferson last week?

Man, she had gotten him good.

"Have a seat."

It had to have been the prank. Maybe putting a fake snake in his car had been too much.

"What's up, Captain?" She plopped into one of his chairs. A feeling of dread began to creep over her. Maybe she actually was in trouble.

He settled in his chair and pulled it forward, his round belly pressed up against the desk. "I have an undercover assignment for you."

At least she wasn't in trouble.

"Captain, with all due respect, you know I was planning on going on a vacation soon."

"Liv, I need you for this one. No one else will do." He adjusted his glasses and handed her pictures of a crime scene. "Bill Sullivan was shot and killed in his barn last night in Unity, Maine. He was an Amish man in his fifties. Someone outside the community reported this."

Shock ricocheted throughout her system. A crime in Unity? Her heart sank, even if she had never really liked the man much. "I knew this man when I lived there. He was my father-in-law."

"I'm sorry," Branson said.

"We weren't exactly chummy, but still..." She stared at the photos in disbelief, dozens of questions spiraling in her head. Liv had never witnessed any violence in her community except for her husband's abuse and the arsonist who had killed her family. Usually Amish communities were peaceful, but sometimes criminals or rowdy teenagers liked to take advantage of the fact that the Amish didn't report crimes like vandalism or arson...or murder.

Was the rest of the community all right? Had anyone else been injured?

Wait...*no!*

"You want me to go there, don't you?" She was ready to argue her way out of this one. She slammed her palms down on his desk as she stood. "You know I never want to go there ever again."

"Liv, calm down. I know it's against the Amish way to give police any information. But we need to find this killer, and you grew up

Amish. If I send any of my other detectives there, they'll stand right out. Besides, they don't know anything about the Amish, and they won't be able to blend in unnoticed. I need you to go there and act like you're one of them again. The killer won't even know the crime was reported or that we are onto him. Can't you just ask to rejoin the church?"

"It's really not that simple." She crossed her arms, looked away, and plopped back down in her chair.

"Why not? Just tell them you want to come back like old times."

"I'm shunned. When people leave, they are shunned. That means no one will speak a word to me unless I repent before the church, beg for forgiveness, and act like I sincerely want to become Amish again." She shuddered at the thought.

"Then do it. Whatever it takes. Since the community in Unity won't accept the help of the police or answer our questions, we think the only way to help these people is for you to go there covertly and investigate without them even knowing it. And the killer will have no idea. No one from their community even reported this crime or planned to. An outsider found out through some gossip and reported it. One of the customers of the community store."

"I know they don't ask the police for help. They believe everything is God's will, and they leave the vengeance to Him. I'm just not sure they'll welcome me back as easily as you think they will."

"Come on. Aren't they nice, forgiving people?"

"They are, but..." She shut her eyes and saw the flames engulfing her home with her parents and siblings dying inside. The arsonist was never found. The elders had told her not to report the crime or look for the man who had murdered her family because their way was to forgive and move on.

But she had held on to the bitterness. She couldn't forgive the killer.

And now she had to go back there? To the place where her family had been killed and her husband had abused her?

Her heart clenched at the thought of returning to her hometown. She hadn't been there in six years. And she had not left on good terms. It wouldn't be as easy as Branson thought it would be. She couldn't just waltz into the community and ask to be forgiven for leaving, could she?

And for killing Jake in self-defense? She didn't think so. All those memories would come rushing back, and it would be too much to deal with. Bile rose in her throat at the thought of returning.

"I can't do this, Captain. I'll do anything else. Send me on a dangerous mission. I don't care. Just don't make me do this. Please." She leaned forward in her chair, put her nice face on, and pleaded with wide-open eyes. "I'd rather run through gunfire than go back there. I'd rather die."

Branson shook his head firmly. "Don't be so dramatic, Liv. If you want your vacation time—if you want your job—you have to do this."

"My job?" A feeling of dread and panic settled over her. Her job was everything to her. She had no life outside of work.

"Look, Liv. Our funds have been reduced, and we have been forced to make cuts. You're a great detective, but you're one of the newer ones. Some of our people have been here ten or fifteen years or more. The board would probably pick you as the first to go if we have to lay people off. So if you do this mission and prove yourself worthy, you would make them reconsider."

She'd rather rot in jail than go back there. She scowled.

"Olivia. I need you to do this."

She gave him a sideways look.

"I'll give you an extra week of vacation time if you go tomorrow and stay until this killer is caught."

"Seriously?" Her eyebrows rose as her interest piqued.

"Don't you go telling anyone. Consider it a bonus for a job well done. I don't know much about what your history is with that place. I'm sorry if this is personal, but don't let it be. Just do your job, and you'll be on the beach sipping a margarita before you know it."

"I don't drink."

"Whatever. Just imagine this—two weeks in the Bahamas, and you don't have to talk to me the entire time."

She nodded slowly, smiling. Sounded like paradise. "How'd you know I want to go there?"

"I've got ears everywhere." He chuckled and leaned back in his chair.

Jefferson must have talked to him.

"Okay, fine. If it will help save lives and catch the killer, I'll do it."

"One more thing. Isaac Troyer, a thirty-year-old Amish man, was also attacked last night. Blunt force trauma to the head. He had traces of wood in his wounds, which were from whatever he was rendered unconscious with." He slid another photo toward her.

Isaac? Her mind screamed at the image of the man she had once loved. She jumped back from the photo as if she had been burned on a hot wood stove.

"He was then left on one of the lanes in the community near his house until a Sid Hoffman brought him to the local hospital. Since this happened on the same night as the murder, we think he was possibly a witness to the crime. You need to covertly protect him, since the Amish won't accept police protection, and he could be the perp's next target. The thing is, Troyer has localized amnesia. He can't remember what happened the night he was assaulted, but keep asking him questions without being obvious. Once you take him home, he might remember more of what happened."

Could this get any worse? She had to take Isaac back to Unity and protect him? Him of all people?

How was she going to act normal around him, try to get

information from him, and protect him during what would be the most awkward encounter of her entire life? She had asked him to run away with her and leave the church, but he had refused and broken her heart. Spontaneous butterflies erupted in her stomach at the thought of him, but she ignored them.

How would he react to her?

The last time she had seen him she had kissed him. Right after her husband had died. After that, he had testified on her behalf during her trial. The jury had acquitted her, finding she had acted in self-defense once they saw the evidence—her bruised neck and other injuries, some of which were older and had not properly healed. Because she had left the church after Jake's death, she had reported what had happened to the police herself, knowing she'd be found innocent.

After the verdict, she hadn't had the courage to speak to him. All she had been able to do was give him a small smile, silently thanking him for testifying before a swarm of news reporters surrounded her, all wanting more details about the Amish woman who had killed her husband in self-defense.

"What's the matter? You know him too?" Branson asked.

"Yeah, I do."

"Are you okay?"

"Yes, Captain."

"You sure? Anything I should know about?"

"I dated him a long time ago when I was a teenager. That's all."

"Okay, that actually works in our favor. Since he is a potential witness, we need you to go talk to him. If he is still single, rekindle your relationship with him—whatever it was you shared—and drive him back home. The closer you get, the better. Stick to him like glue. If he is a witness, he needs your protection."

Like glue? Really? She let her head drop in her hands dramatically.

"Okay, Liv?" Branson prodded, leaning forward and slightly raising his voice.

"Okay." She sighed heavily.

The Bahamas would have to wait.

"Hey, this is none of my business either, but I know a little bit of what happened there, how you killed your husband in self-defense."

"Yeah. I did."

"Why? What did he do? If I may ask."

Could he get any nosier?

"After abusing me for three years, he tried to choke me to death, so I stabbed him," Olivia said emotionlessly. "I had no choice. The community didn't report it. I did, because I knew I was innocent. And the jury and judge agreed once they saw the evidence and heard the testimonies." She stood up and walked out of the office, leaving her boss wide eyed.

Buy Undercover Amish here: https://www.amazon.com/Undercover-Amish-Covert-Police-Detectives-ebook/dp/B01L6JE49G

About the Author:

Ashley wrote her first manuscript at age fourteen and self-published her first book at sixteen. She wrote this book at age twenty. She wrote seven manuscripts before the age of twenty-five and became a bestselling author at age twenty-five.

She lives in Maine where she lives with her husband, daughters, and son and will be releasing several more Amish books over the next few years.

Ashley loves hearing from her readers. Please find her on Facebook by searching for "Ashley Emma, author/editor" or email her at **amishbookwriter@gmail.com**.

Sign up to get free Amish eBooks at ashleyemmaauthor.com.

A review on Amazon.com would be greatly appreciated!

Praise for *Undercover Amish*

"*Undercover Amish* is the first Amish novel I've read, and I have to say it was a fascinating and insightful look into a different culture. Ashley Emma clearly did extensive research on the subject and portrayed this group in a compassionate, thoughtful manner. Couple her careful handling of this society with her compelling characters and heart-racing plot, and you've got a real winner!"

--Staci Troilo, author of *Mind Control, Bleeding Heart* and many other titles

"What can I say, I LOVE mysteries! I love getting to know the characters, their motivations and then trying to figure out the outcomes. I am therefore delighted to have discovered *Undercover Amish.* Not only does the main character, Olivia, has a unique background of being Amish, but the trajectory of her life from that background to becoming a policewoman is fascinating and totally unexpected. Not only did I find myself engrossed in the unraveling of a crime, but also in the learning about a culture, within my own country, about which I was, admittedly, basically ignorant. Kudos to Ashley Emma for creating this wonderful series. I can't wait to read more of them!"

--Leslie K. Malin, LCSW, psychotherapist, iLife Transition Coach, and author of *Cracked Open: Reflections on the Transformative Power of Failure, Fear, & Doubt* website/blog: http://www.JustThinkn.com

"*Undercover Amish* is a suspenseful, realistic work of fiction. Ashley weaves two opposite worlds together in a fast-paced story following Detective Olivia Mast. Olivia's journey forces her to face issues of identity, rise up to work challenges, and eventually she finds love. It's an easy read that will keep you guessing until the end."

--J.P. Sterling, author of **Ruby in the Water**

"Buy this book! It's a five-star read in my opinion. Whether you have ever read Amish detective stories before or not, I know you'll like this one and be totally engaged from start to finish. The characters are well-developed, unique, quirky, and three-dimensional. I enjoyed the author giving her readers an inside view of the Amish community, especially during dangerous and unpredictable times. I eagerly await the sequel to this novel!"

--Wendy Pearson, moderator of **The Write Practice**

"I love a good mystery and this one has an interesting storyline. A relatively short read and kept me engaged and trying to guess the next twist. This is the kind of book I love to have when traveling or for an afternoon at the beach."
--C.L. Ferrari, bestselling author of **Enriching Your Retirement**

"Ashley Emma has crafted an intriguing crime mystery with a surprising twist. I didn't see that ending coming at all. And I'm a little jealous. Once I got into this book, I couldn't put it down."

--Michael Wilkinson, bestselling author of **A Father's Guide to Raising Daughters**

"I really enjoyed this book, right through the last page!! Undercover Amish is a compelling read that will keep you going until the very end! The only disappointing thing for me about Undercover Amish was when the story ended—I already miss the main characters!"

--Sue M Wilson, author of **Home Matters**

www.suemwilson.com

"This book will take no time at all to grab you and take you into a world most of us know nothing about. Because the author spent time with the Amish, Ashley Emma is able to present her story in a truthful manner. After you read this, you will feel as though you know enough to say you understand them. (You may even find yourself wanting to wear more solid colors.) But murder has crept into their safe haven. Olivia, the main character, who was once Amish comes back and investigates a string of crimes, all while being undercover. I highly recommend this book. Ashley keeps you on the edge of your horse and buggy seat while making you fall in love with her characters. You'll be sorry once it is over. Thankfully there are more of her books to read coming soon!"

--Emily L. Pittsford, author of A Most Incredible Witness

Ashley's Amish Adventures: An Outsider Living with the Amish | Ashley Emma

(Below is a photo of some quilts for sale in a shop in Lancaster, Pennsylvania. They sell for about $1,000. Aren't they amazing!? Read the sequel *Ashley's Amish Adventures: Attending an Amish Wedding* to read about my return to Unity and when I visit an Amish family in Pennsylvania!)

www.ingramcontent.com/pod-product-compliance
Lightning Source LLC
Chambersburg PA
CBHW020415080526
44584CB00014B/1344